VERA MERCER
NEW WORKS

EDITED BY MATTHIAS HARDER

DCV

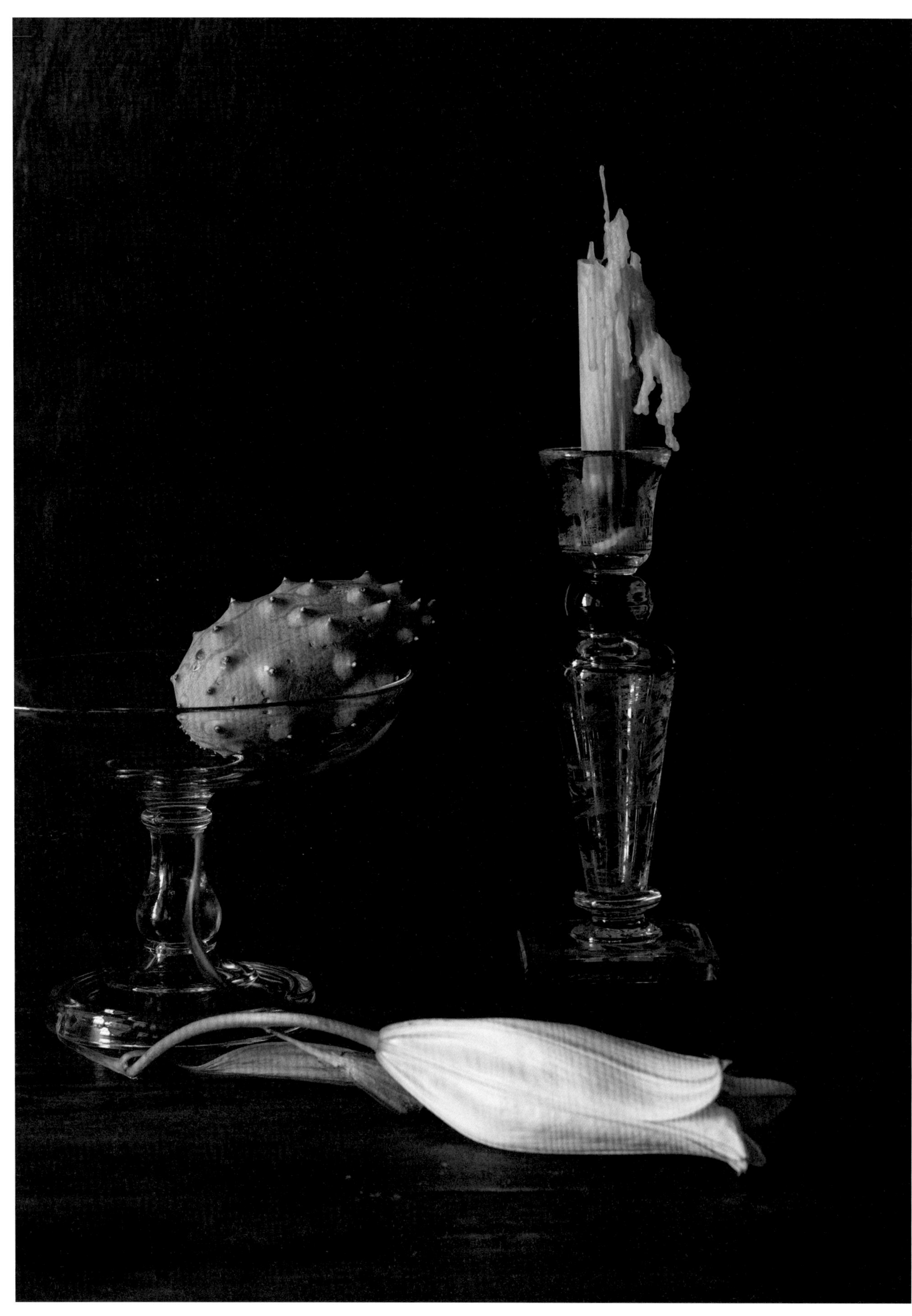

Matthias Harder

NEUE ARBEITEN

Vera Mercer bleibt sich treu in ihrer stilllebenbasierten Fotografie, die sie in ihren Wohnorten Omaha und Paris in immer neuen Arrangements realisiert. Doch parallel zu den farbigen, großformatigen Inkjet-Prints stellt sie seit 2018 auch kleinformatige Platinum-Prints her. Sie hat entsprechende Kurse besucht, sich von Experten beraten lassen – und kommt nach relativ kurzer Zeit zu erstaunlichen eigenen Bildfindungen in einer großartigen Printqualität.
Die historische Platinum-Printtechnik ist vergleichsweise aufwendig, sie wurde in den 1870er-Jahren entwickelt und erfreute sich in der Folge insbesondere bei den Piktoralisten größter Beliebtheit, also um die Wende zum 20. Jahrhundert. Zunächst muss ein Papier mit verschiedenen Chemikalien getränkt und getrocknet werden, bevor es durch ein Negativ belichtet werden kann. Anschließend wird es in einer weiteren chemischen Lösung inklusive Platinsalz entwickelt und gut gewässert. Verschiedene Zusätze erzeugen unterschiedliche Tonungen. Das reiche Tonwertspektrum ist eine der Besonderheiten dieser fotografischen Drucktechnik. Charakteristisch für das Edeldruckverfahren sind auch die schwarzen, unregelmäßigen Ränder oder Flächen rund um das eigentliche Motiv. Von den meisten Fotografen, die auch heute noch mit diesem Bildgebungsverfahren arbeiten, werden die Ränder durch ein Passepartout abgedeckt. Vera Mercer hat einige ihrer Platinum-Prints mit, andere ohne diese gewissermaßen ausgefransten Bildkanten hergestellt. Sie bewahrt sich in ihrem Werk stets eine gedankliche und künstlerische Freiheit, das gilt auch für ihre Platinum-Prints, die wir erstmals in dieser Publikation reproduziert sehen können.

NEW WORKS

Vera Mercer continues to create compelling still life photographic works, which she realizes in multifaceted arrangements at her homes in Omaha and Paris. Parallel to her colorful, large-format inkjet prints, she has also been producing small-format platinum prints since 2018. In a relatively short amount of time, she studied the technique, gathered expert advice, and has succeeded in creating stunning images as high-quality prints.
The historical platinum print technique is a fairly elaborate one. Developed in the 1870s, it subsequently enjoyed great popularity, especially among the Pictorialists, around the turn of the twentieth century. Platinum printmaking involves first infusing a sheet of paper with various chemicals and allowing it to dry, before being exposed through a negative. The image is then developed in another chemical solution that includes platinum salt, and well rinsed. Different additives produce different tones; the rich tonal range is one of the special features of this photographic printing technique. Black, irregular borders around the image are also characteristic of this high-quality printing process. Many of the photographers still working with this imaging technique today cover the edges with a passe-partout. Vera Mercer has produced some of her platinum prints with these borders, others without. Each and every work is approached by the artist with a sense of open-mindedness and artistic freedom – and this also applies to her platinum prints, which we can see reproduced in this publication for the first time.
Some of Mercer's platinum prints could be described as minimalist in terms of their motif, depicting a single blossom or bud against a neutral background or on a silver plate. Through the narrow framing, a cabbage head or a pear can seem almost

Manche von Mercers Platindrucken sind sehr reduziert, sie zeigen nur eine einzige Blume oder Blüte vor einem neutralen Hintergrund oder auf einem Silberteller; ein Kohlkopf oder eine Birne werden von ihr durch den engen Bildausschnitt geradezu monumentalisiert. Die Gesamtkomposition bleibt vergleichsweise flächig, ein Aspekt, der uns bereits in Mercers früheren Blumenbildern begegnete. Andere Platinum-Motive wiederum sind Varianten oder schwarz-weiße Übersetzungen ihrer farbigen Blumenstillleben. Motivisch identisch, ist der Eindruck der verschieden großen Aufnahmen sehr unterschiedlich, denn im Gegensatz zu den Farb-Inkjets wirken die getonten Platindrucke eher abstrakt und zeitlos.

Doch auch die neobarocken Farb-Stillleben entstehen weiterhin parallel, einige fallen jedoch inzwischen etwas düsterer und morbider aus als noch vor einigen Jahren. Wir finden die gleichen Ingredienzen wie in ihren früheren Arrangements: Gläser und Vasen, Früchte und Pilze, Silberbesteck oder tote Tiere, mal frisch erlegt, mal steht eine übrig gebliebene Hülle stellvertretend für eine verstorbene Kreatur. Zudem arrangiert sie Kerzenständer mit frischen oder fast heruntergebrannten Kerzen, dazu immer wieder Blumen, die teilweise schon Blütenblätter verlieren. Doch während manche der toten Tiere auf den Stillleben weiterhin aussehen, als würden sie schlafen, muten andere eher an, als wären sie gerade exhumiert worden; so entstehen neue, radikalere Vanitas-Studien zwischen Schönheit und Vergänglichkeit, diesem immerwährenden Dualismus in Vera Mercers Werk.

Die Welt wird bei Vera Mercer zur mal reduzierten, mal überbordenden Kulisse – und immer zu einer Art Schaukasten. Formal sind ihre Bilder Jagdstillleben oder flämischen Küchenstücken des 17. Jahrhunderts nicht unähnlich, doch in der zeitgenössischen Fotografie sind sie unvergleichlich. Hervorzuheben ist die ihr eigene irritierende Kombination von Vorder- und Hintergrund, bei der die Größenverhältnisse völlig verschoben werden: Großformatige, nahansichtige Fotografien mit riesigen Blüten kontrastieren beispielsweise mit dem davor arrangierten neuen Stillleben. Ihr Werk ist insofern auch ein verwirrendes Spiel mit der Realität. Ebenfalls charakteristisch und autonom ist die Illumination der Szenerie mit Kerzenlicht. Dass manche Accessoires ein wenig aus der Zeit gefallen wirken, fügt den Stillleben eine weitere inhaltliche Ebene hinzu; denn sie finden sich tatsächlich zuhauf in den beiden Wohnungen der Fotografin und geraten so selbstverständlich von ihrem Leben in ihre Bildwelt. Insofern sind die Fotografien auch eine Art Selbstporträt von Vera Mercer.

Die Fotografin verwendet für ihre Werke die modernste Kameratechnik mit bis zu Millionen Pixel pro Aufnahme und parallel begeistert sie sich für eine Bildtechnik aus der Pionierzeit des Mediums; der jeweils mehrstufige Kompositionsprozess läuft

monumental. The overall composition remains comparatively flat, an aspect we can encounter in Mercer's earlier images of flowers. Other platinum motifs are variations, or black-and-white interpretations, of her colorful floral still lifes. Despite sharing identical motifs, each of these variously sized photographs creates a unique impression. In contrast to the color inkjets, the toned platinum prints appear more abstract, heightening their innate sense of timelessness.

Mercer continues to produce her colorful neo-baroque still lifes, although some are now somewhat darker and more somber than they were a few years ago. Elements from her earlier arrangements occur here as well: glasses and vases, fruits and mushrooms, silverware, or animal cadavers, sometimes only recently deceased; occasionally, only the remaining outer shell stands in for the creature itself. Candlesticks also make an appearance, with fresh or worn-down candles, in addition to the ever recurring flower blossoms, which sometimes lose their petals along the way. While some of the animals featured in the still lifes give the impression of merely being asleep, others look as if they were recently exhumed – offering new more radical vanitas studies bridging beauty and transience, the perennial dualism we sense throughout Vera Mercer's work.

Here, the world becomes a backdrop that might be subdued or exuberant – but always a kind of showcase. Formally, her images are not dissimilar to hunting still lifes or Flemish kitchen paintings from the seventeenth century, but in contemporary photography they are unparalleled. What stands out is Mercer's provocative combination of foreground and background, in which proportions are radically shifted. Large-format, close-up images of giant blossoms, for example, are juxtaposed with a new still life arranged in front of them. In this respect, her work is also a confounding play with reality. Her illumination of the scenery with candlelight is a further unique characteristic of her work. Some of the featured accessories seem slightly anachronistic, which contributes another level of meaning to the still lifes. Indeed, many of these relics can be found in both of the photographer's apartments and so naturally pass from her daily life into her pictorial world. In this respect, the photographs are also a kind of self-portrait of Vera Mercer.

Even while using the most modern camera technology with up to a hundred million pixels per shot, the photographer has embraced an imaging technique that dates back to the pioneering days of the medium. Her compositional process goes through a number of stages each time, sometimes planned, sometimes spontaneous. Mercer starts out by obtaining all the elements for her photograph, especially food in its purest form, which is sourced from her local markets. In some cases,she receives props from friends, returning from a hunt. Then she arranges them in compositions, reacting to her source

mal geplant, mal spontan ab. Zunächst besorgt sich Mercer die Bildbestandteile, vor allem Nahrung in ihrer pursten Form, auf Märkten ihrer unmittelbaren Umgebung. In anderen Fällen werden ihr die Requisiten gebracht, etwa von befreundeten Jägern. Auf dieses Ausgangsmaterial reagiert sie intuitiv mit ihren Arrangements. Sie rückt auf dem Kaminsims in Paris oder auf großen Holztischen in Omaha Gläser und Vasen zurecht, drapiert darauf Fische, Schalentiere oder frisch erlegtes Wildbret, ergänzt Früchte, Gemüse oder Pflanzen – bis die Komposition für ihren Blick stimmig ist beziehungsweise sich das erwünschte Drama einstellt, über das die Fotografin einmal in einem Interview sprach. Im nächsten Schritt entstehen die ersten Aufnahmen der Zusammenstellung, digital oder analog, die in der digitalen Dunkelkammer zum finalen Bild weiterverarbeitet werden – bei Nichtgefallen wird der Aufnahmeprozess wiederholt. Die digitalen Bilddaten werden anhand verschiedener Testprints und Bildgrößen überprüft, der lange Produktionsprozess endet mit der Entscheidung für einen bestimmten Bildausschnitt in einem entsprechenden Format. Dieses finale Motiv wird von Vera Mercer schließlich als Exhibition Print oder als signierte und limitierte Edition in kleiner Auflage produziert – alle Zwischenstadien sind nur Makulatur und wandern in den Abfall. Die Platinum-Prints hingegen sind Unikate.
Erst in der Rezeption vollendet sich bekanntlich ein Kunstwerk, denn erst durch das Aufladen mit unseren Emotionen während der Bildbetrachtung, seien sie enthusiastisch oder ablehnend, weitet sich das visuelle Angebot zu einem entsprechend individuellen Assoziationsraum. Und so können wir möglicherweise die Einzelwerke von Vera Mercer in ihrer vollen Sinnlichkeit erfahren, die Wärme der brennenden Kerzen, das weiche Fell mancher Tiere, die schleimige Glitschigkeit eines Oktopus oder den Duft der Blumen.
Ihren Wunsch in Jugendjahren, später als Gärtnerin zu arbeiten, konnte Vera Mercer zwar nicht verwirklichen, aber mit Blick auf die vielen Blumen und Pflanzen in ihren Wohnungen und auf ihren Bildern scheint sich dennoch ein Lebenskreis geschlossen zu haben. Das Gleiche gilt für ihre Rückkehr in die analoge Dunkelkammer, diesen geradezu mystischen Ort der Bildentstehung und Metamorphose, einer Alchemistenküche vergleichbar. Das sehen und spüren wir in ihrer neuen Werkgruppe der Platinum-Prints. So bleibt das Werk von Vera Mercer überaus vielschichtig und autonom, neben den Stillleben entstehen auch weiterhin Porträts oder Mischformen dieser Genres, und das Nebeneinander der verwendeten Techniken ist ebenfalls ungewöhnlich in der heutigen Fotografie.

materials in an intuitive manner. Glasses and vases are placed on the mantelpiece in Paris or on large wooden tables in Omaha: fish, shellfish, or freshly shot game is draped across them. Then come the fruits, vegetables, or plants – until the composition makes sense to her or conveys the desired drama, as the photographer once explained in an interview. In the next step, a digital or analogue camera is used to take the first photographs of the composition. These are further processed in the digital darkroom to produce the final image. If the photographer is not satisfied, the shooting process is repeated. The digital data is evaluated using various test prints and image sizes, and the intricate production process ends when a specific part of the image is selected for print in an appropriate format. This final motif – all of the previous images are intermediate stages and ultimately discarded – is finally produced by Vera Mercer as an exhibition print or as a signed and limited edition in small quantities. The platinum prints, on the other hand, are one of a kind.
Of course, a work of art is not truly complete until it is seen, for it is only by infusing it with our emotions while we look at it – be they enthusiastic or negative – that the visual object expands into an individual associative space. By this process, we can experience each of Vera Mercer's works in their full sensuality – the warmth of burning candles, animals' soft fur, the slick, viscous exterior of an octopus, or the scent of flowers.
Vera Mercer was not able to realize her childhood dream to work as a gardener later on, and yet – seeing the multitude of flowers and plants in her apartments and her photographs – that aspect of her life nevertheless seems to have come full circle. The same applies to her return to the analogue darkroom, an almost mystical place of image creation and metamorphosis, comparable to an alchemist's kitchen. We can both see and sense this in her new series of platinum prints. Vera Mercer's work over the years continues to be remarkably multifaceted and autonomous. In addition to still lifes, she still produces portraits as well as hybrids of the different genres she works with; her juxtaposition of techniques remains exceptional in contemporary photography.

INKJET PRINTS

PARIS AND OMAHA, 2016 – 2021

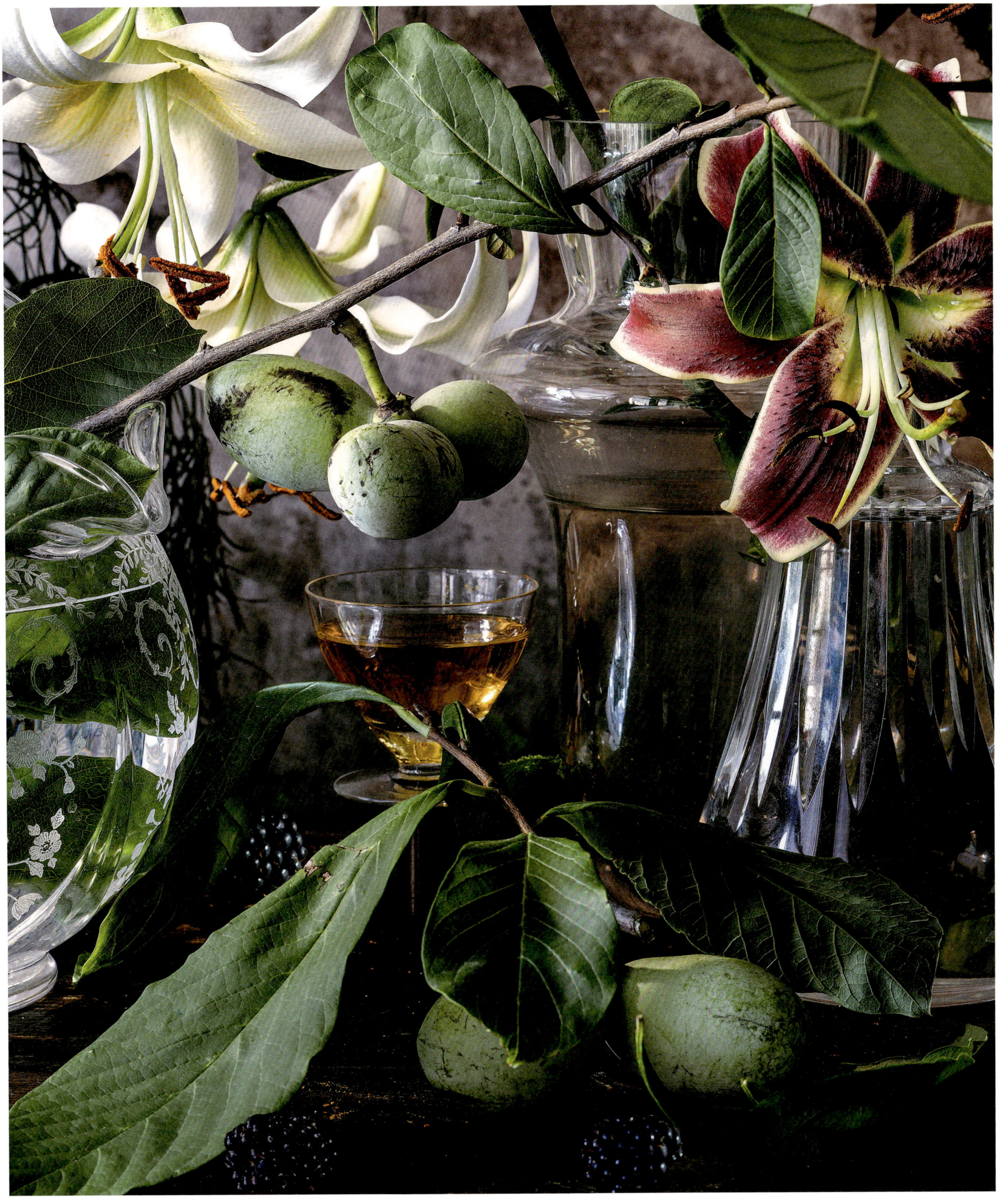

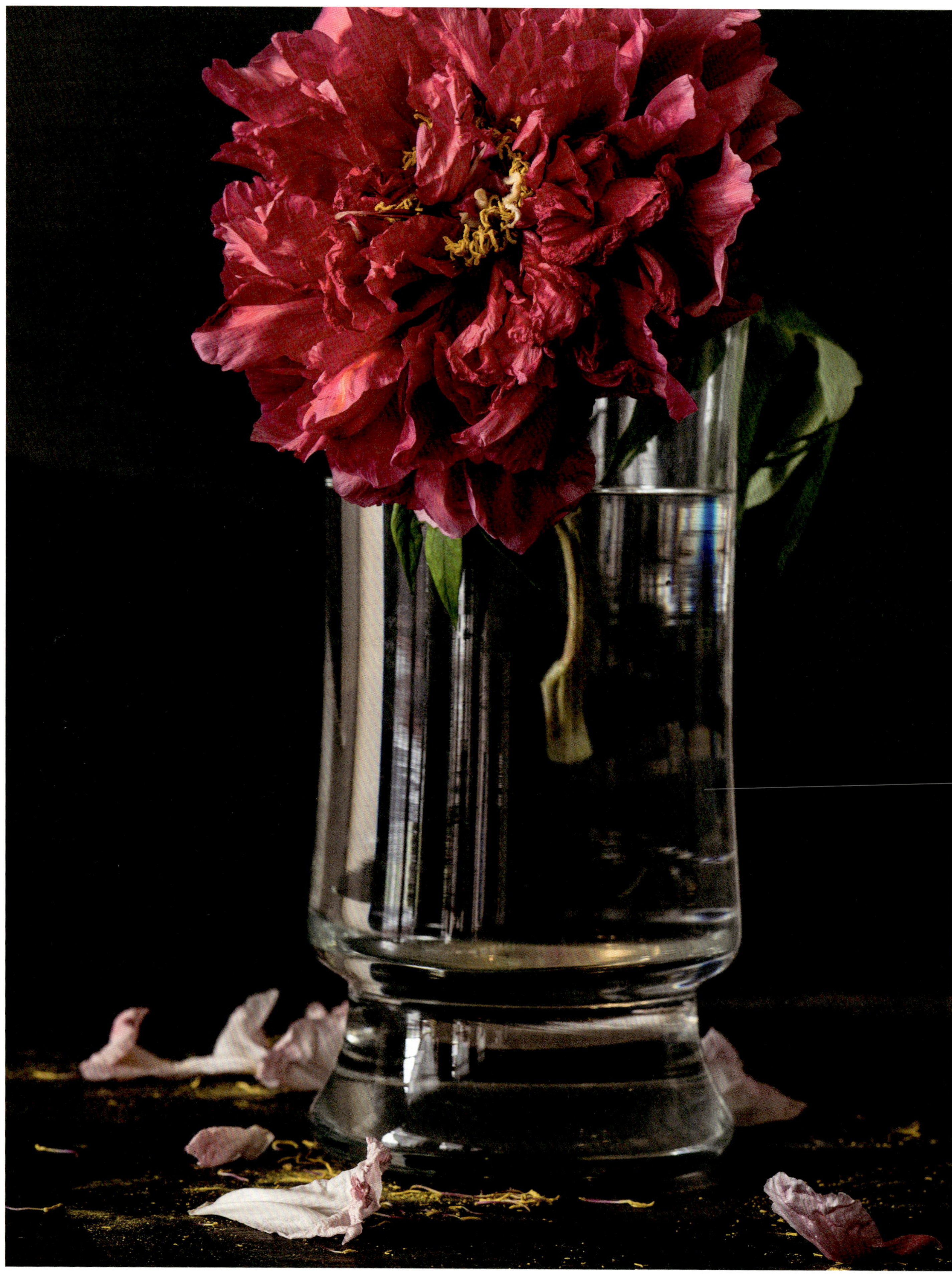

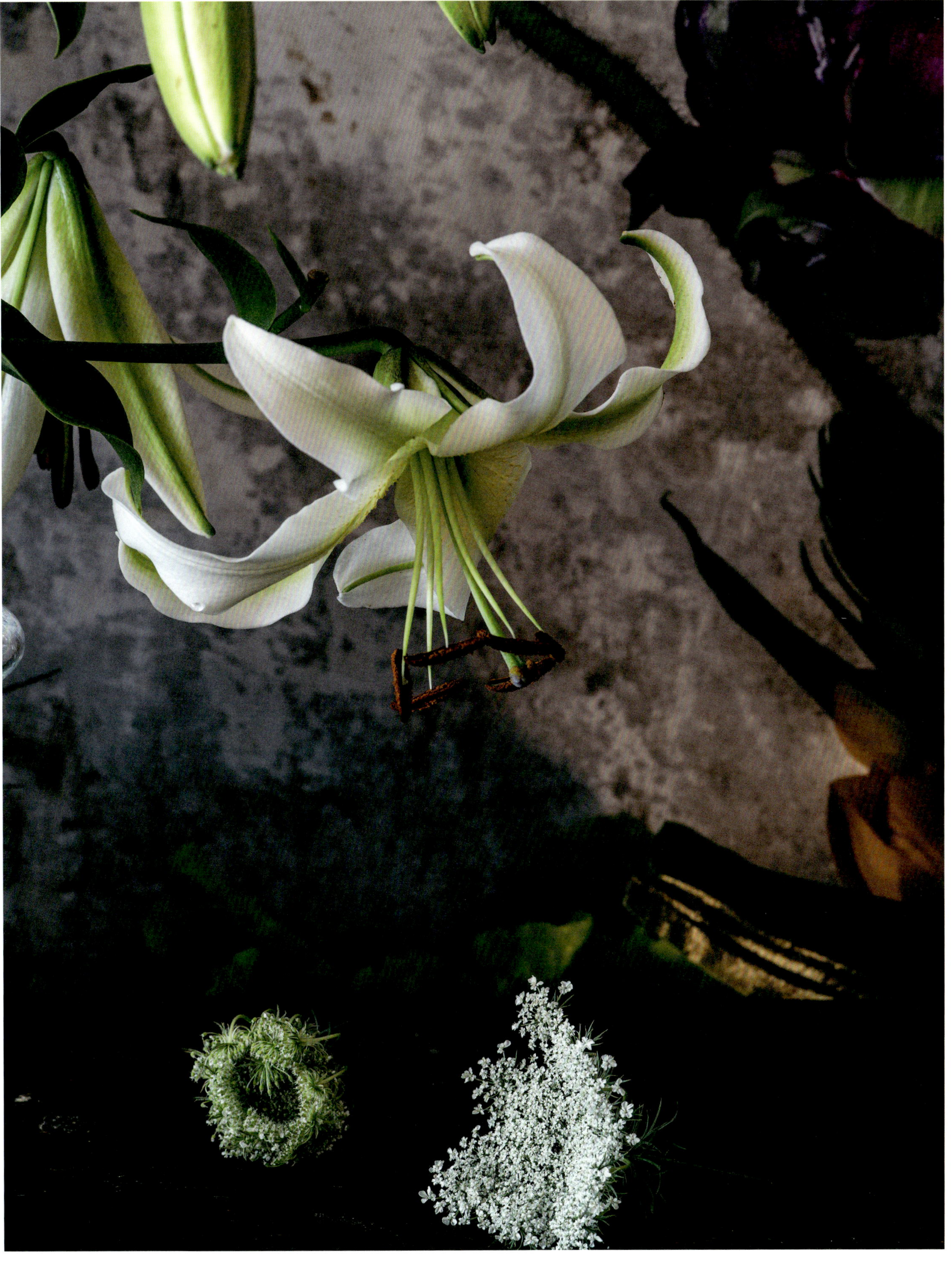

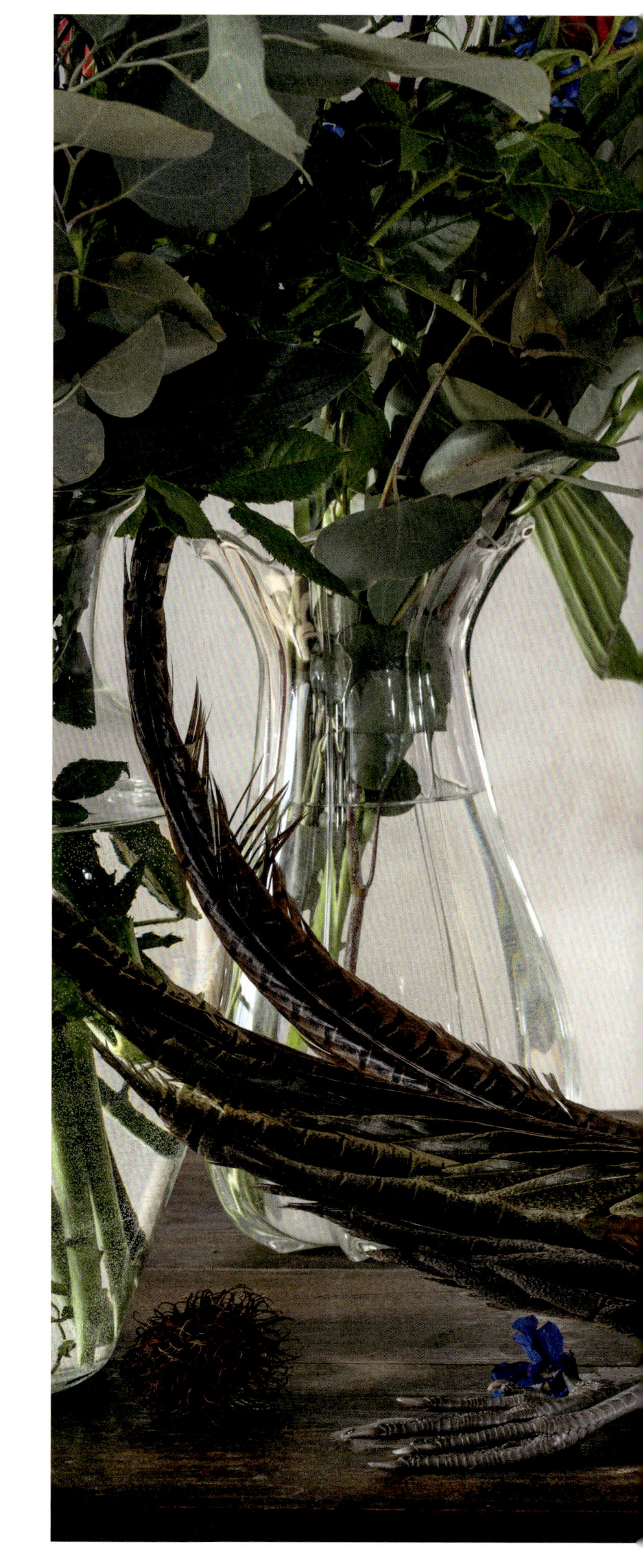

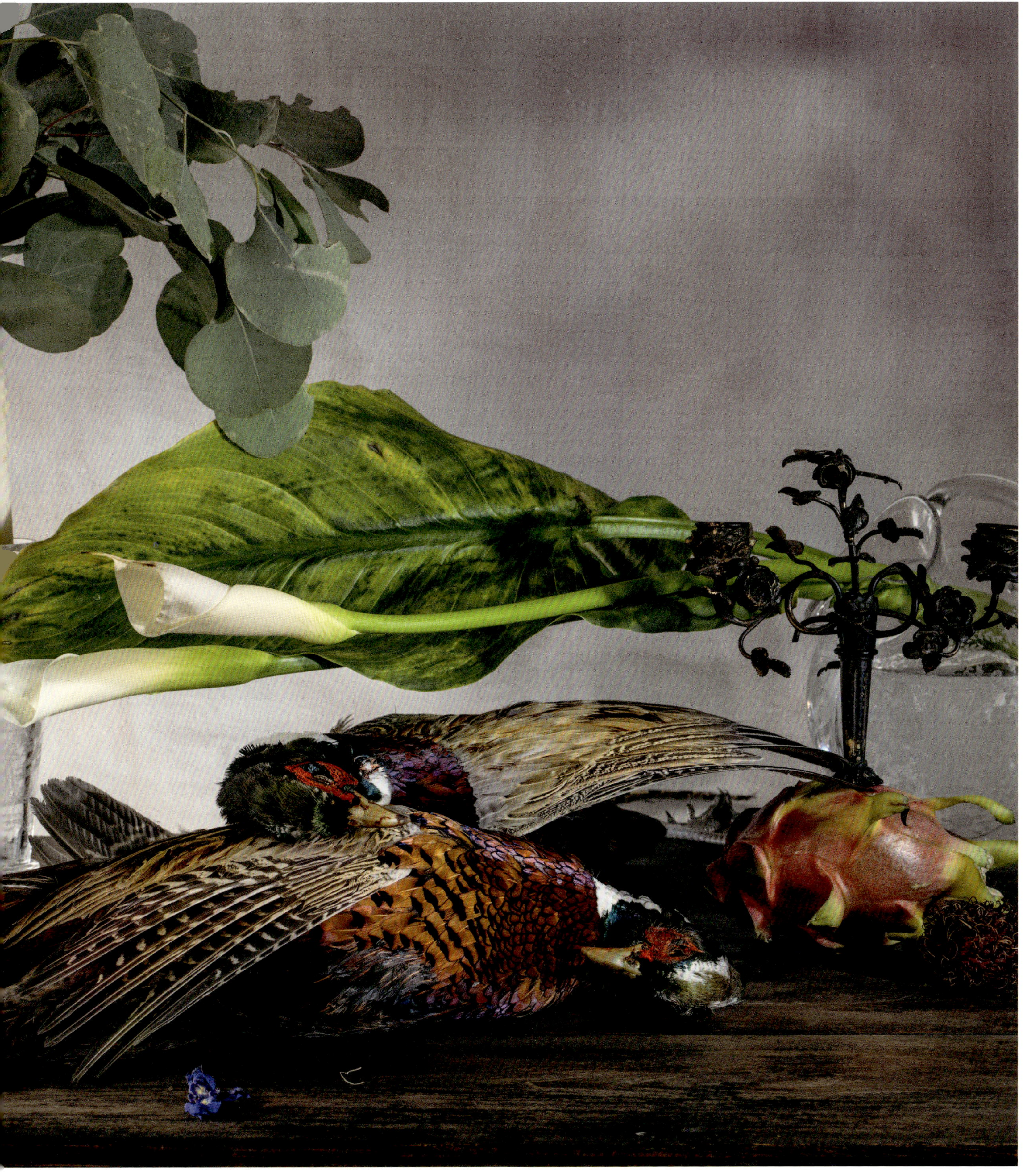

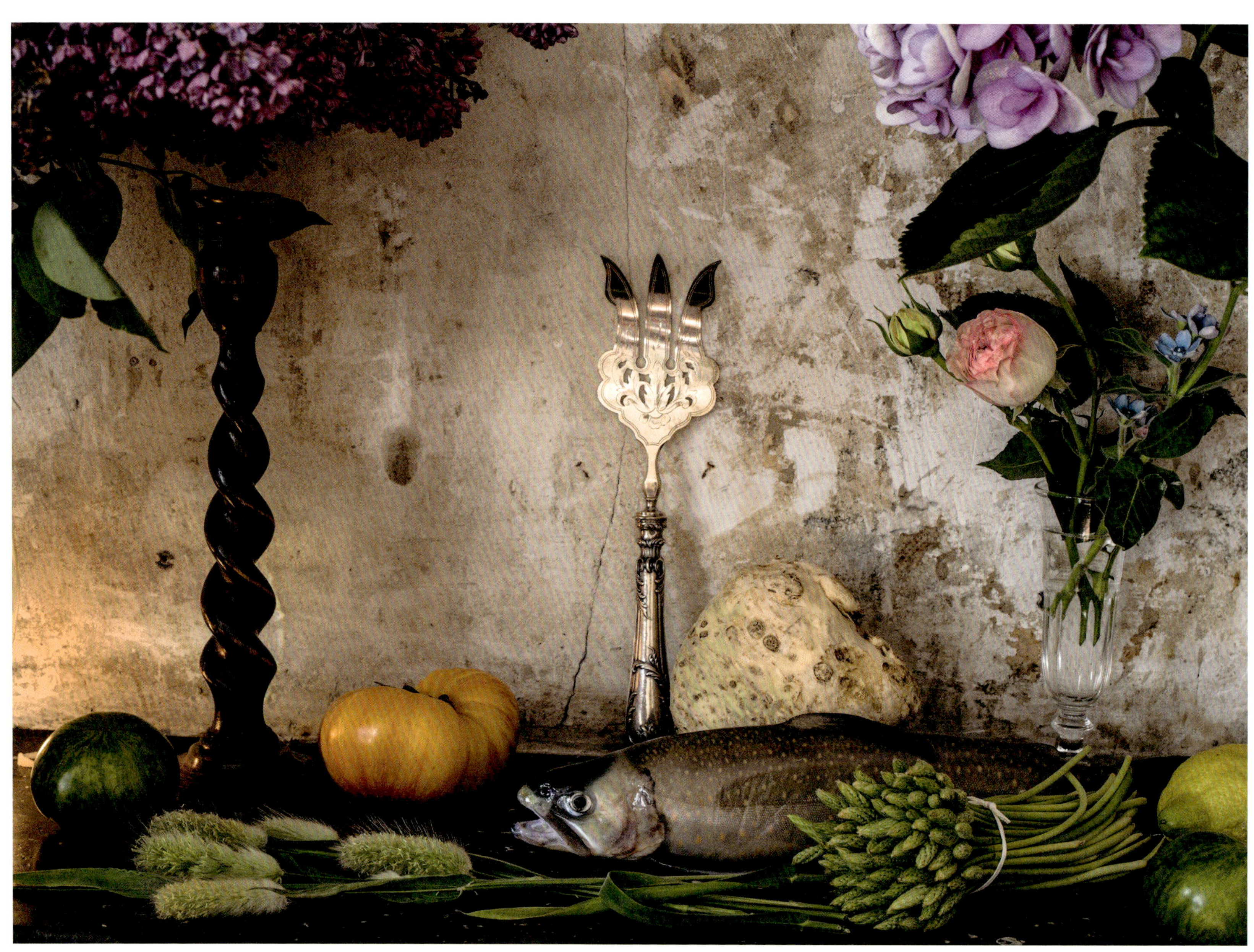

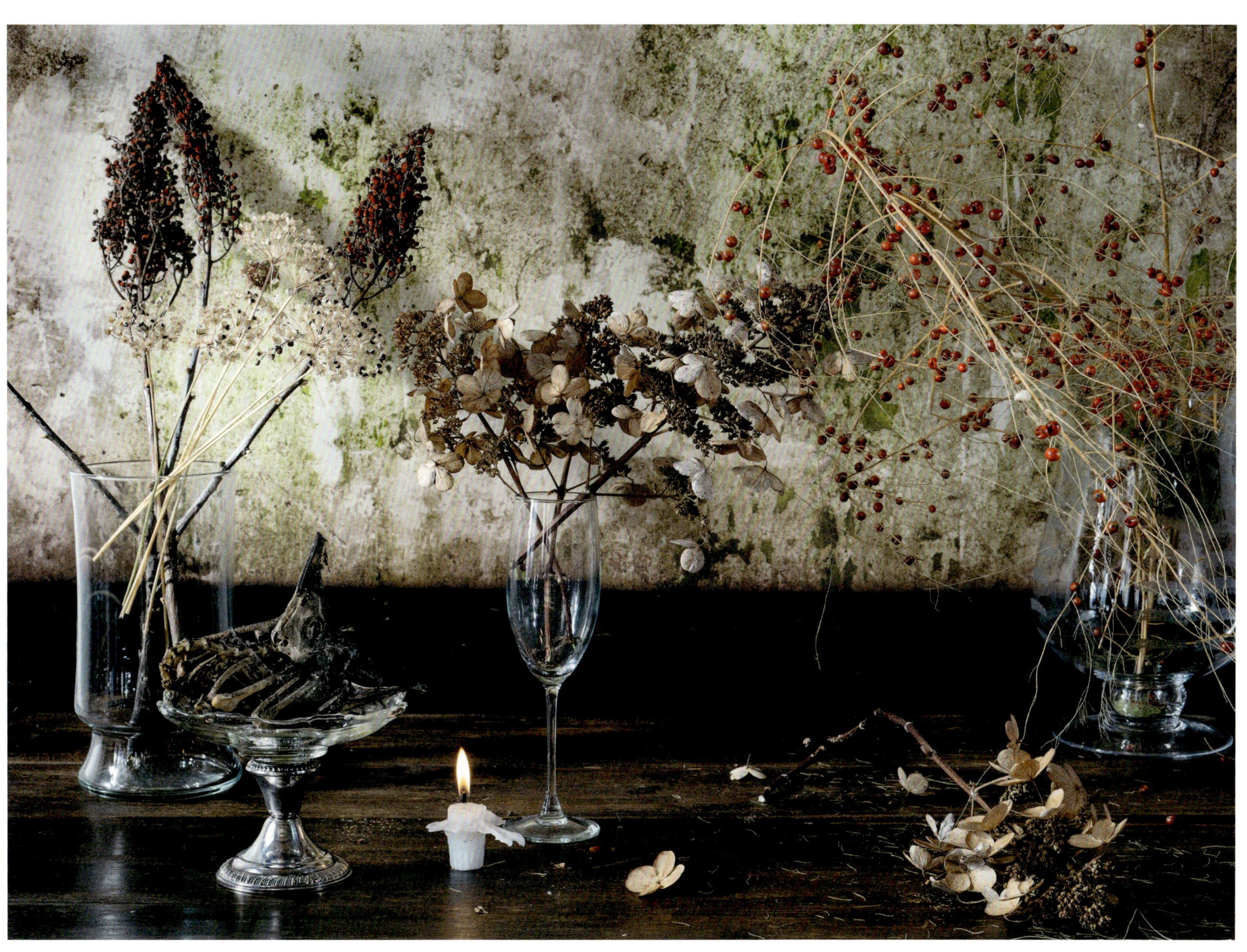

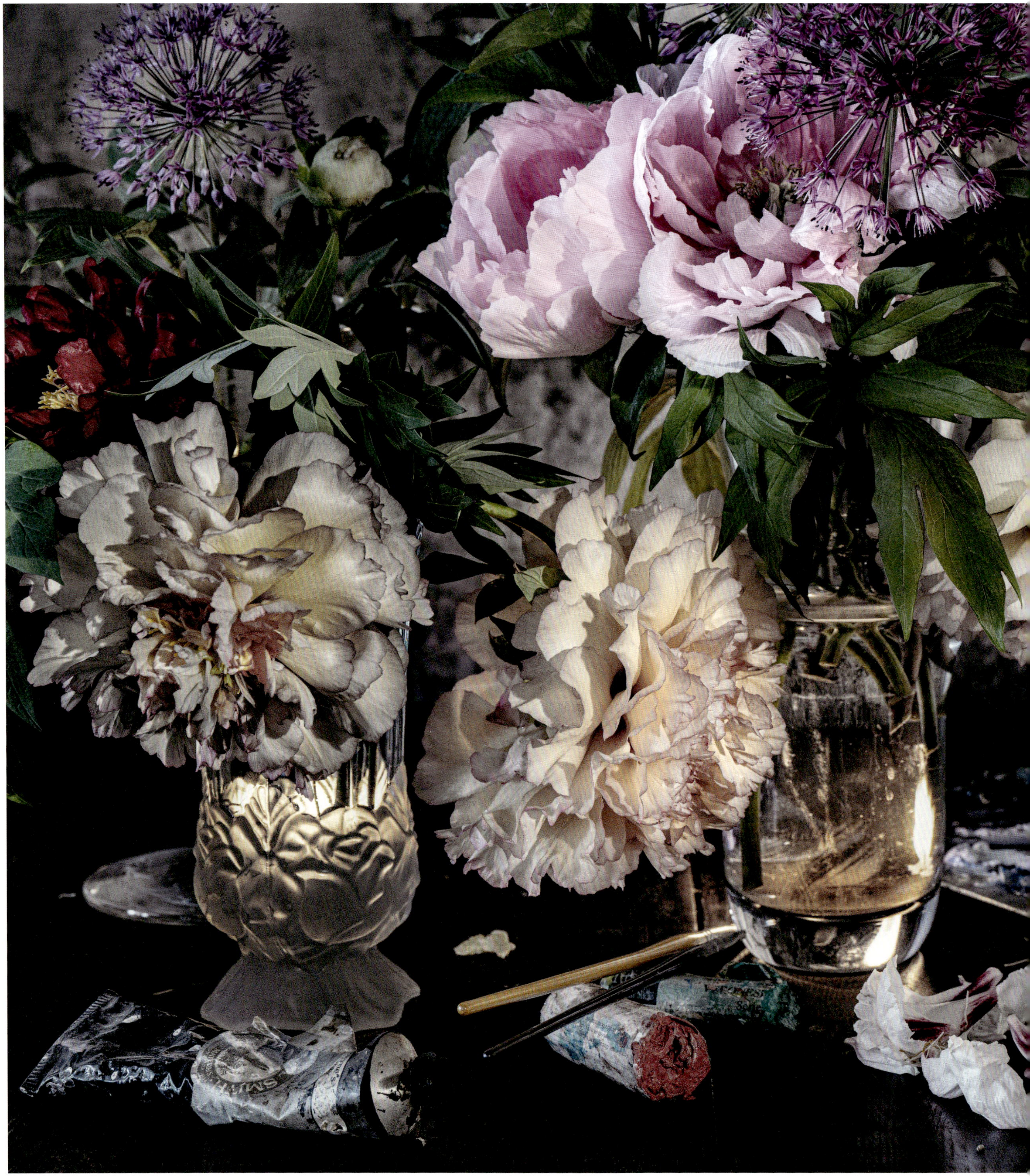

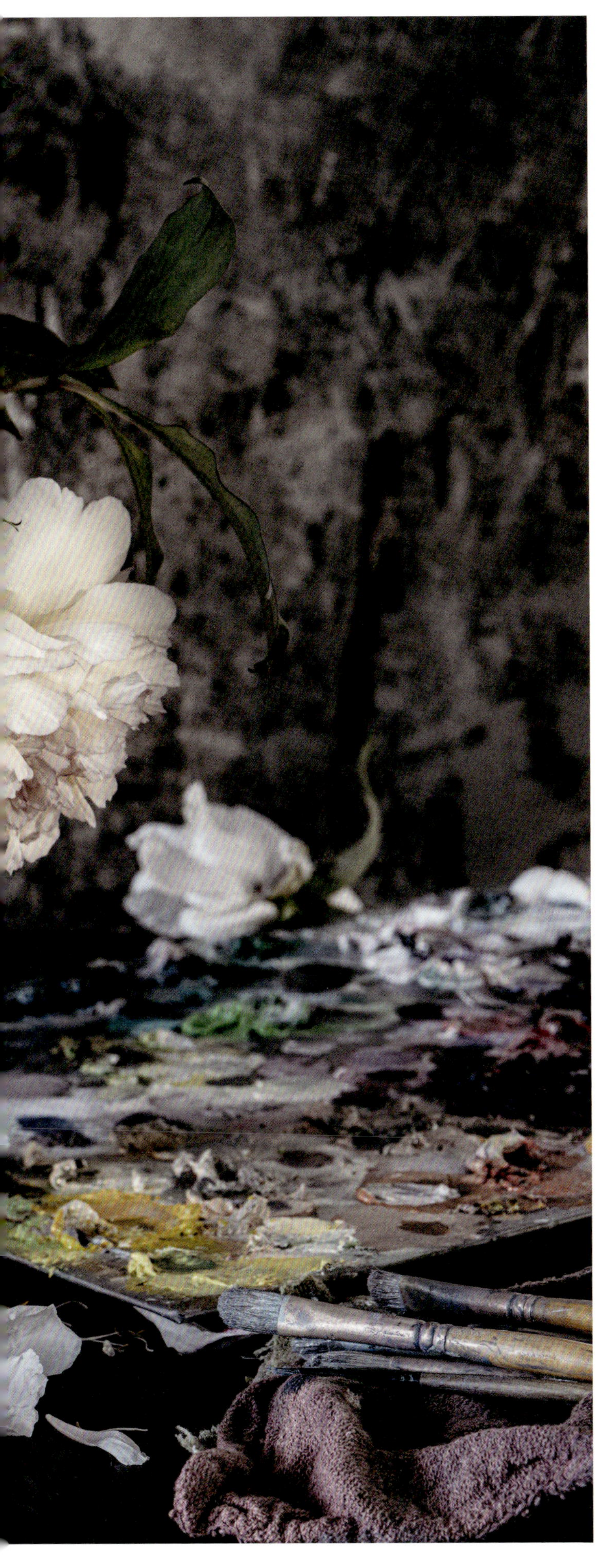

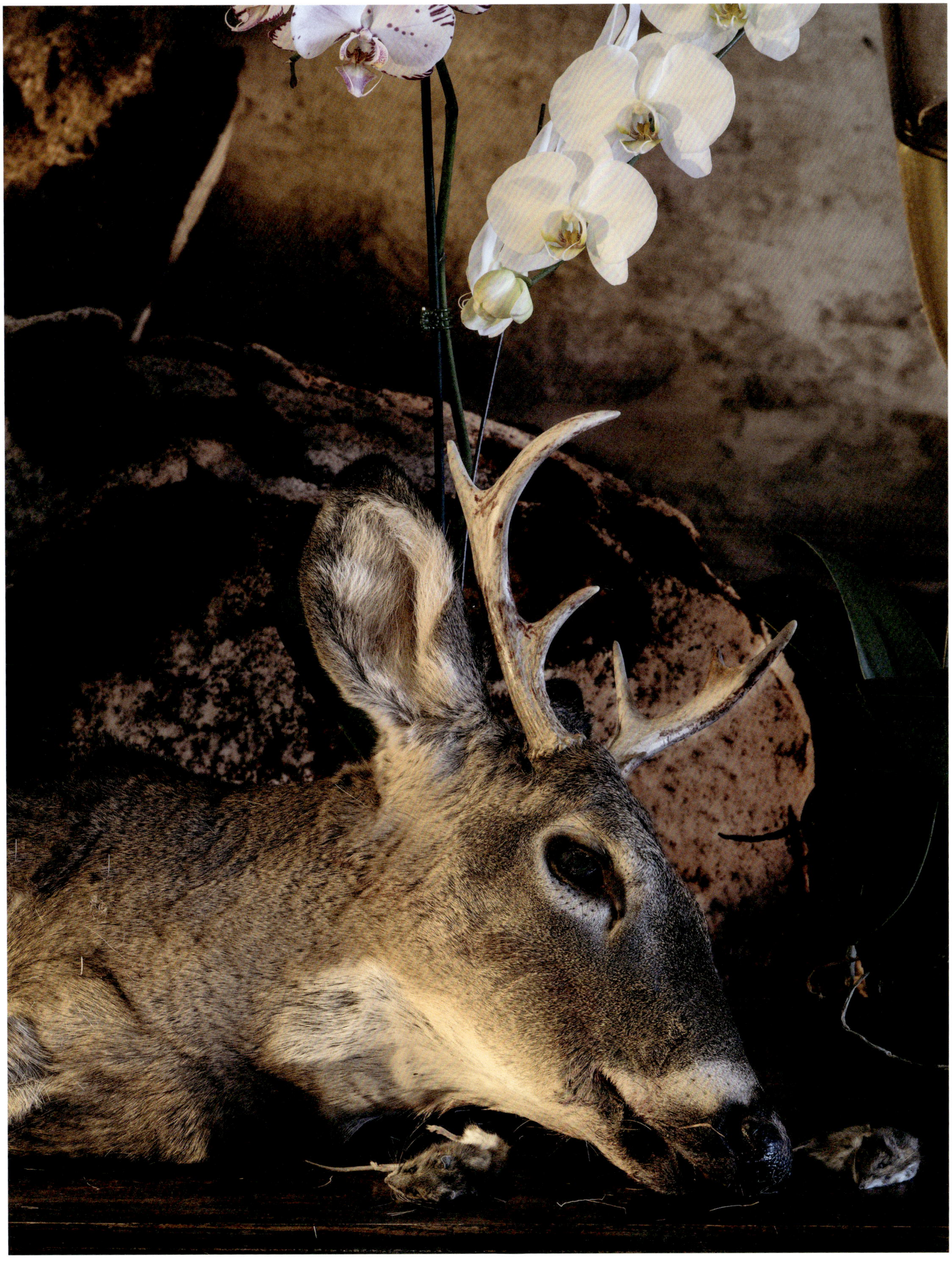

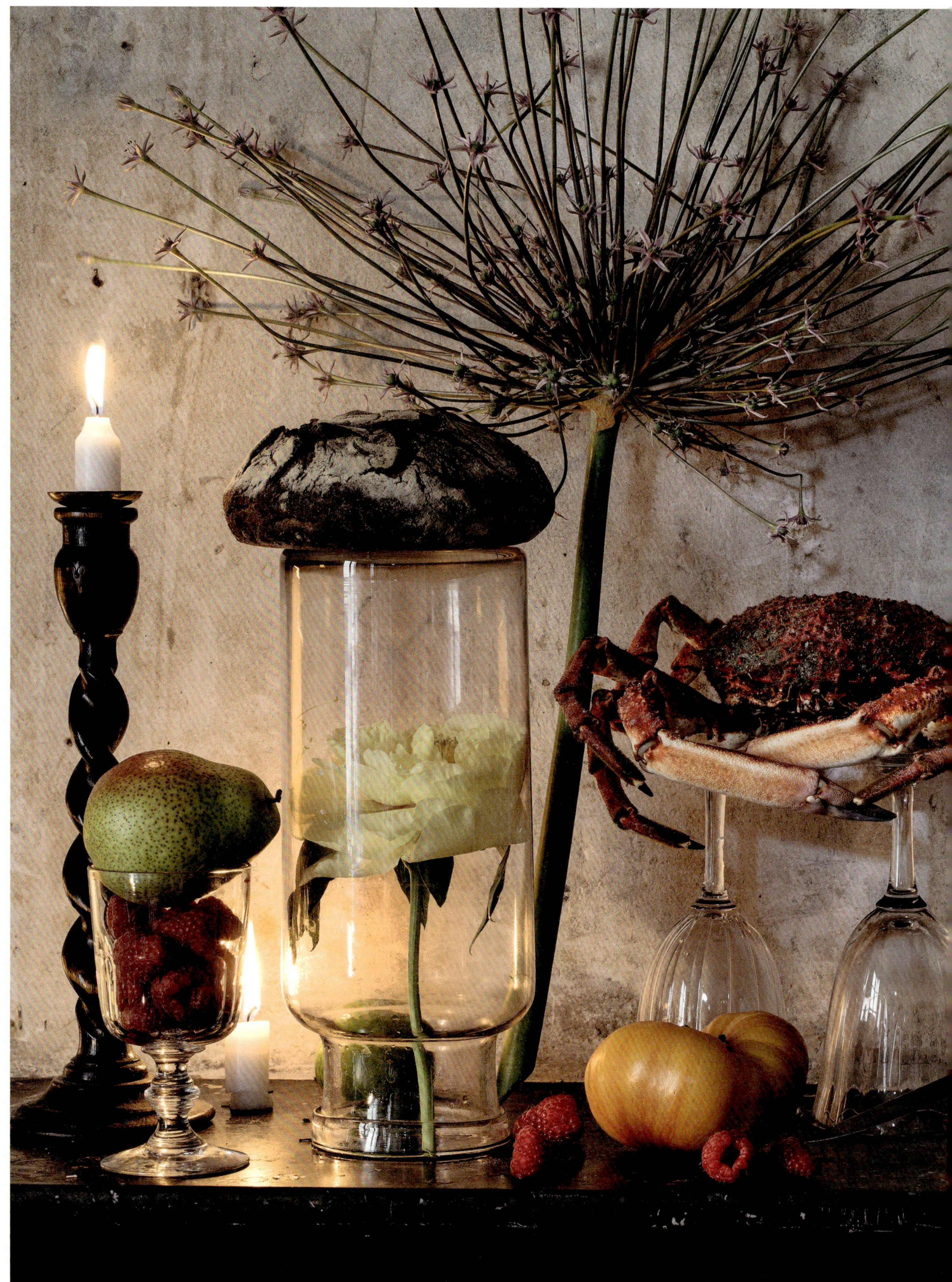

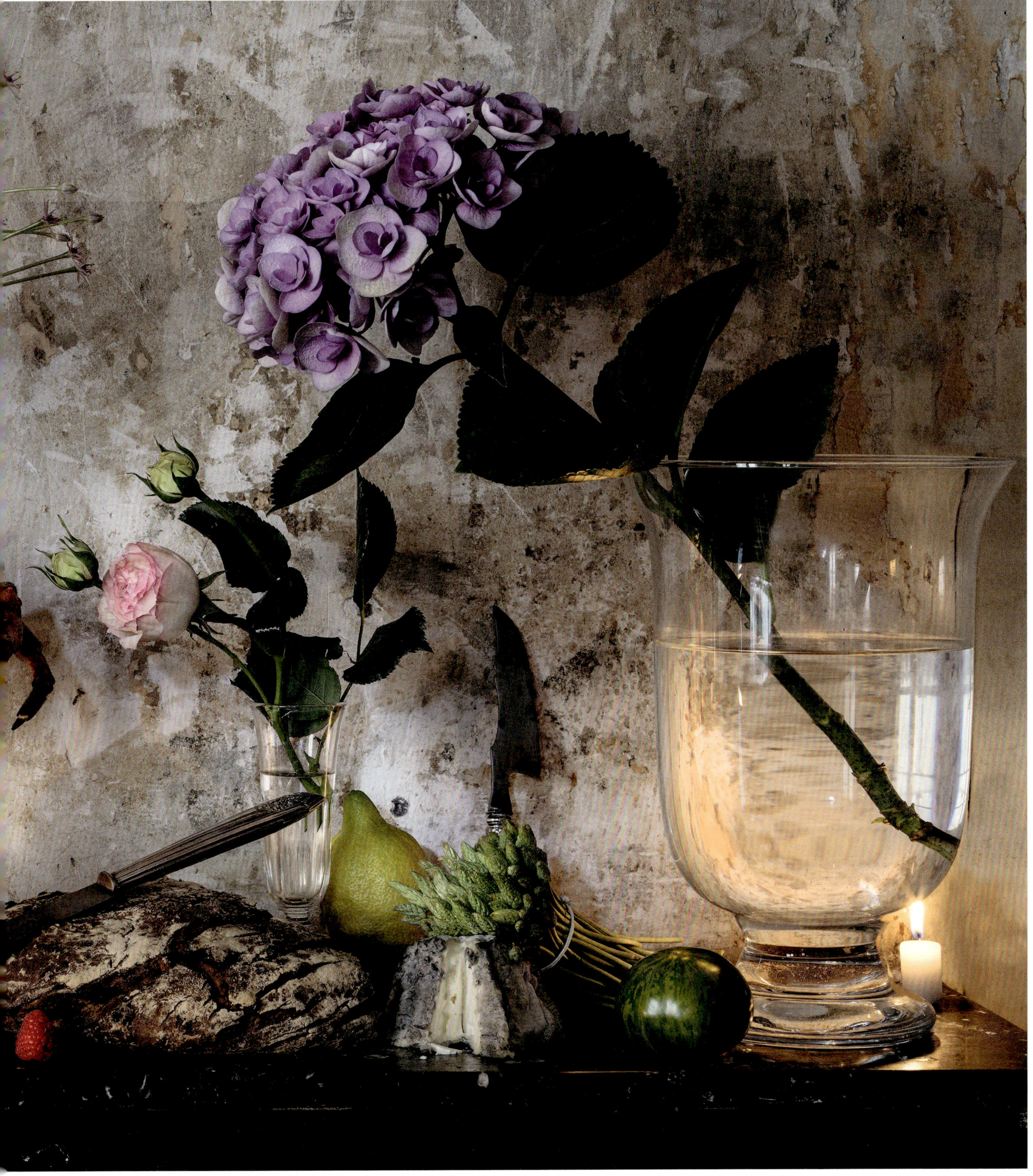

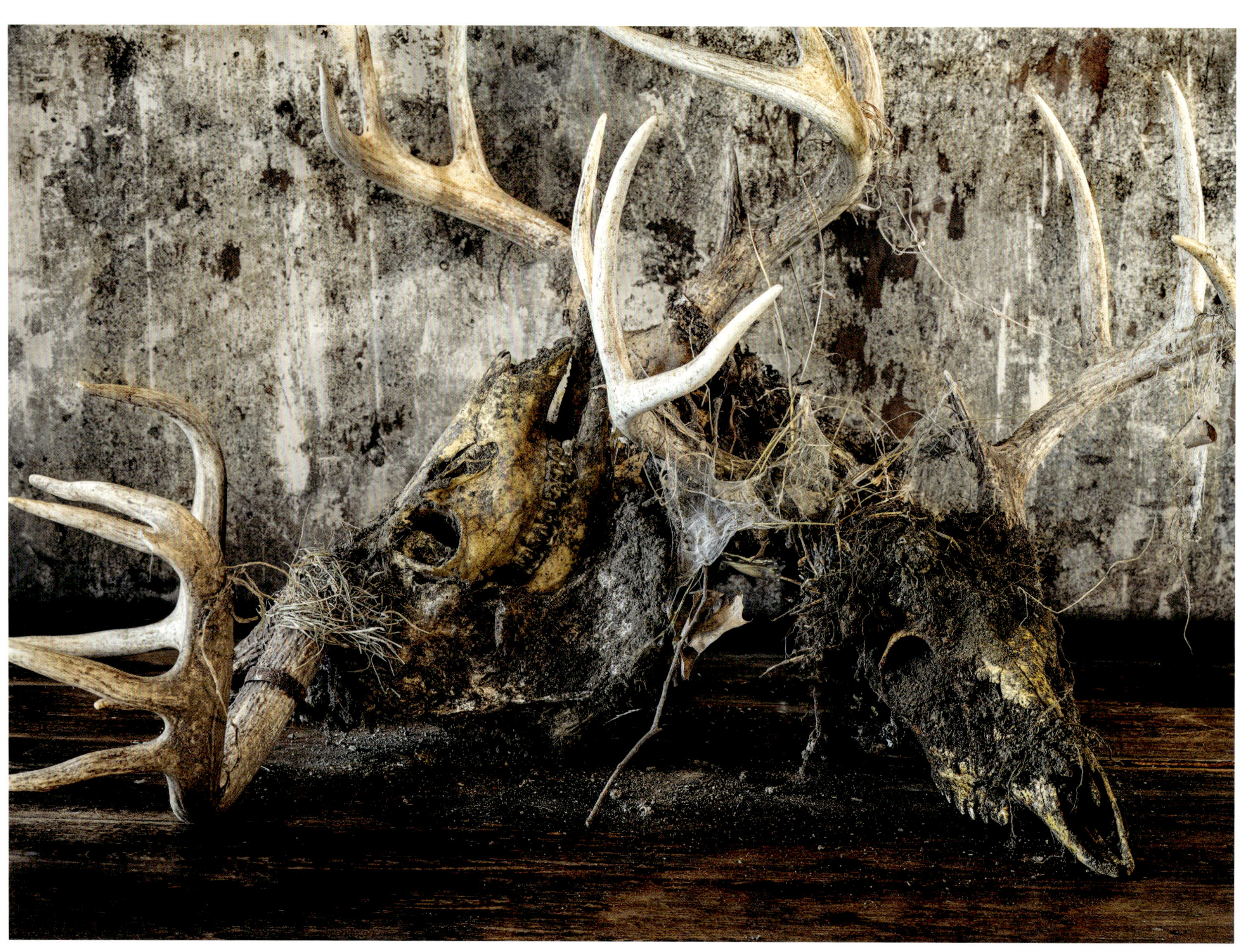

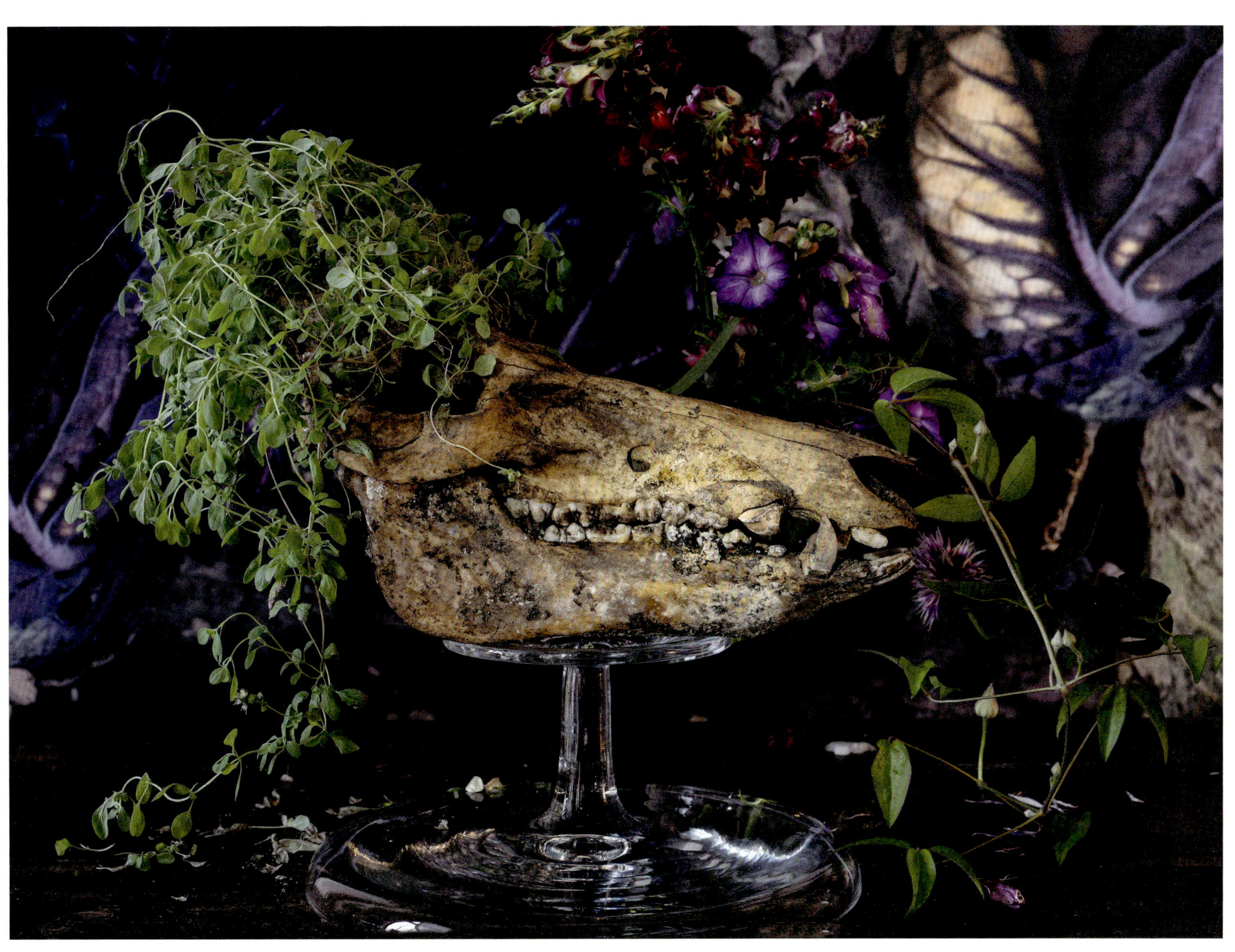

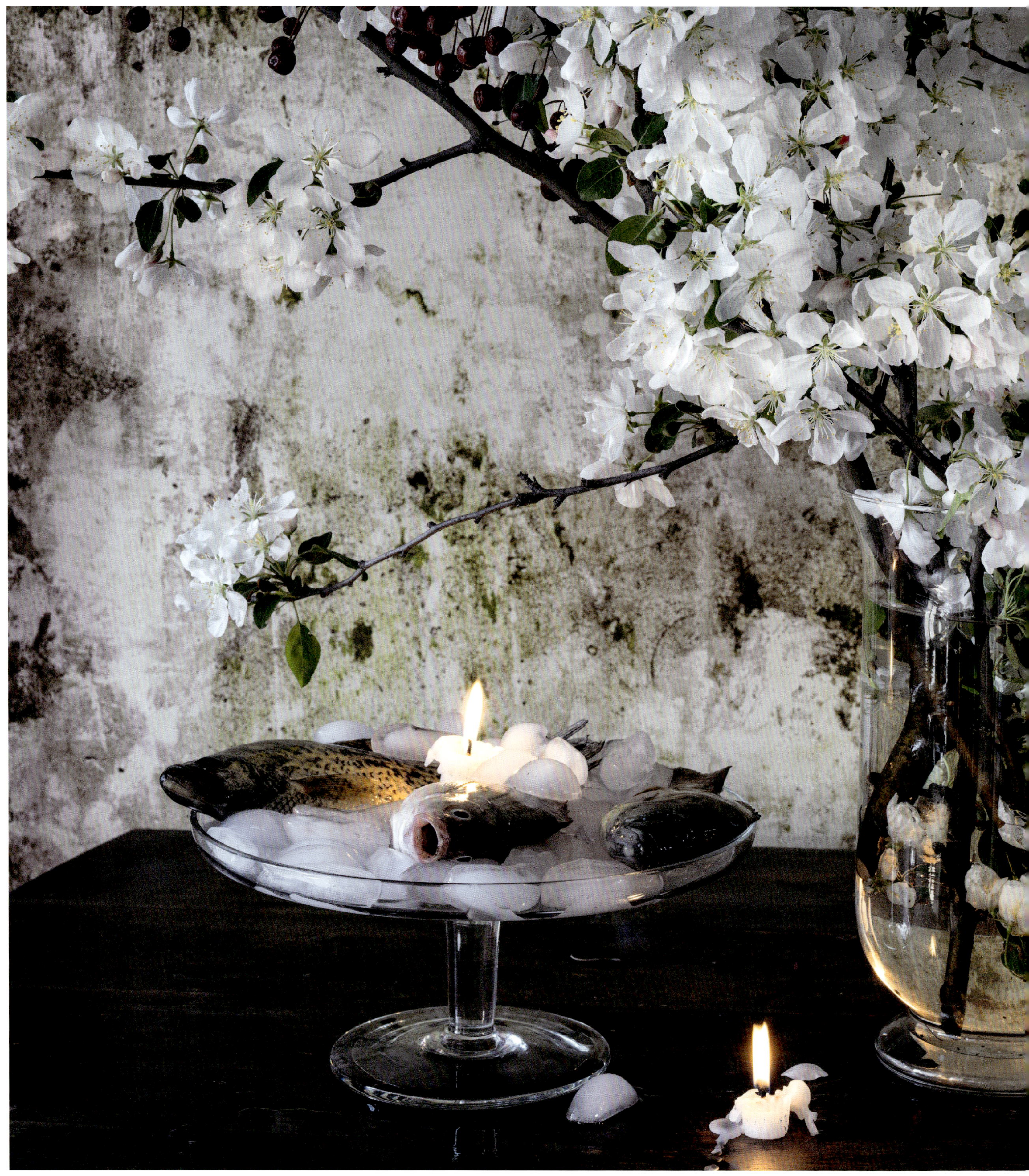

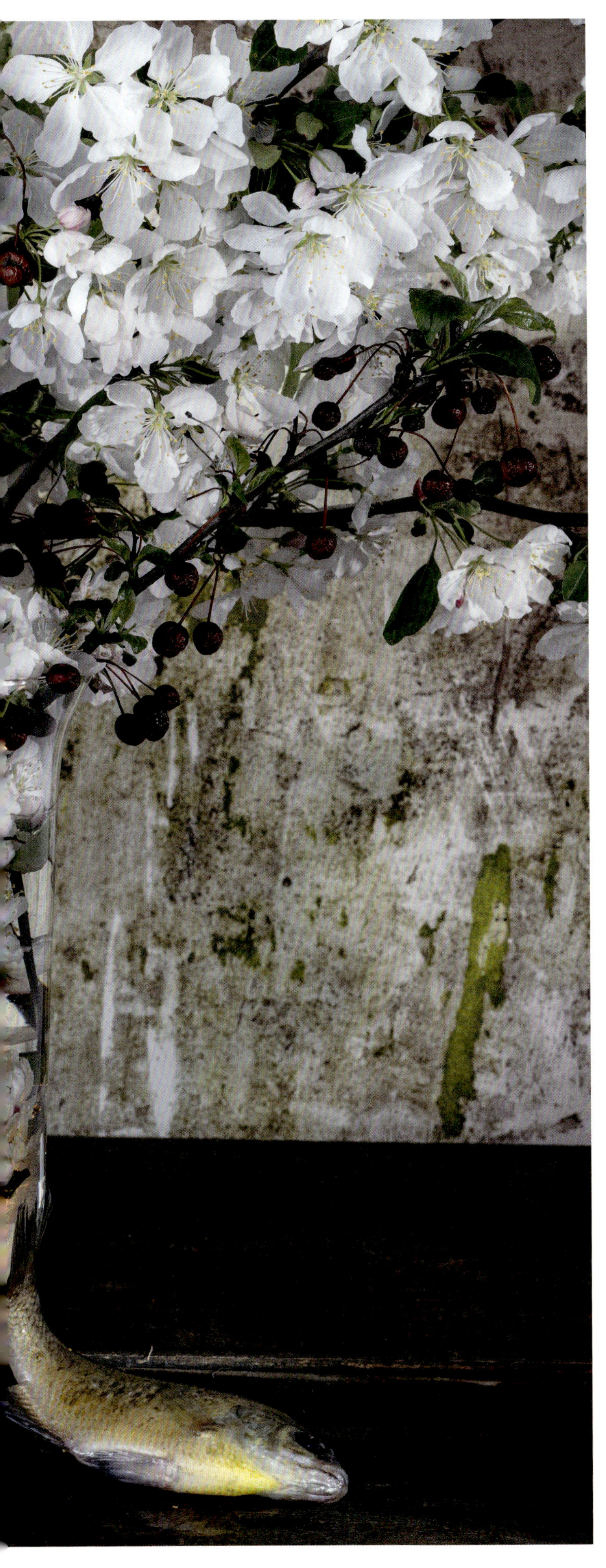

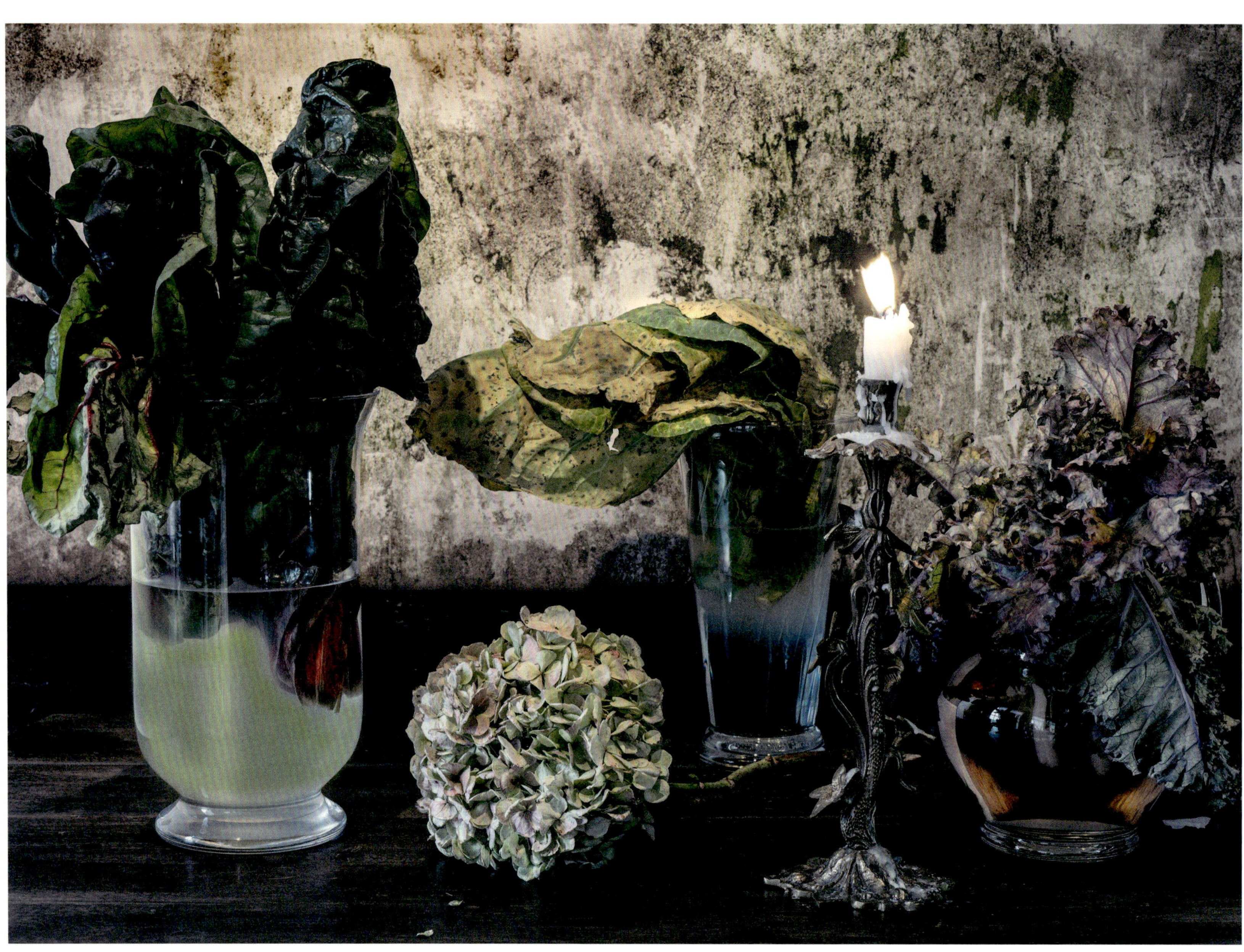

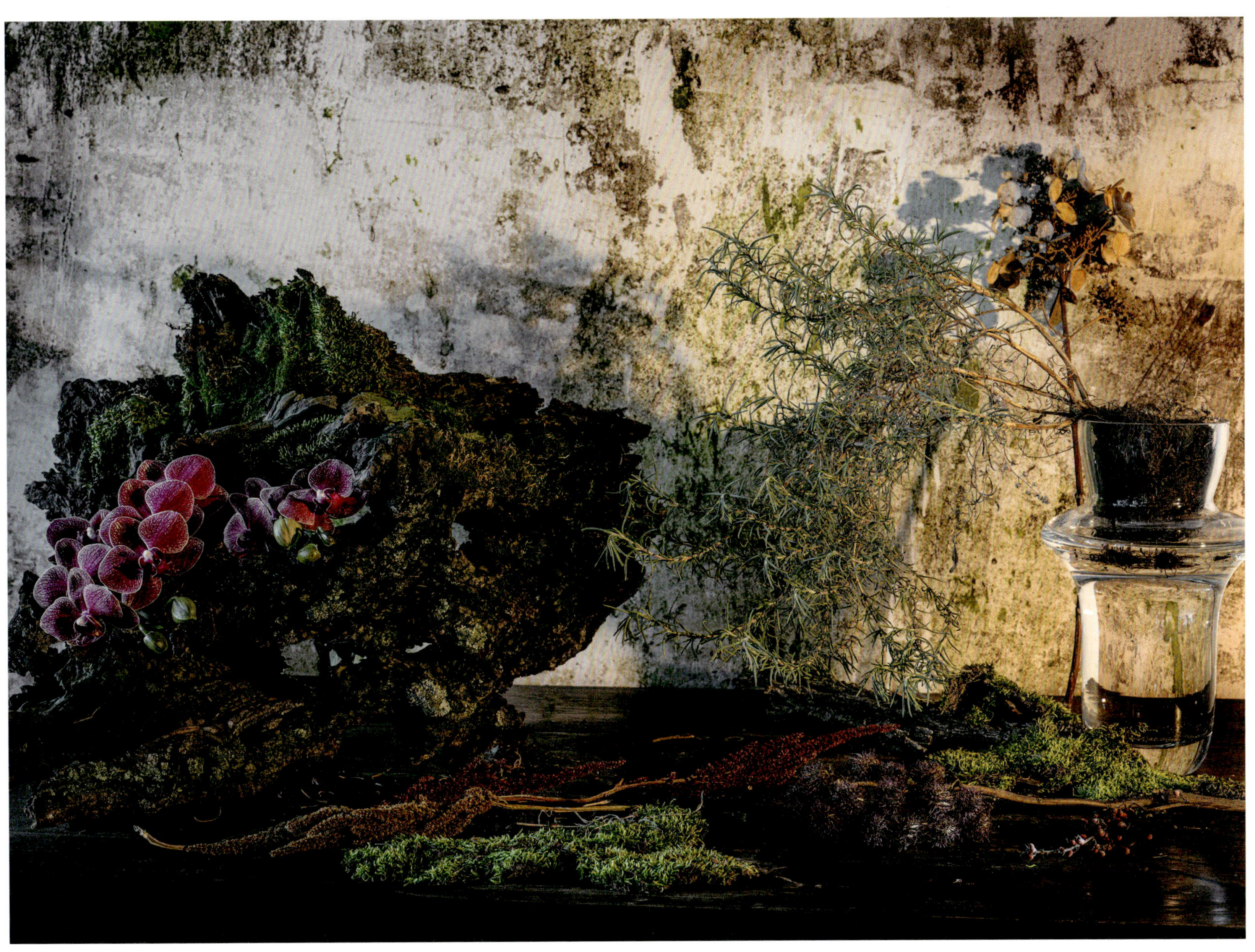

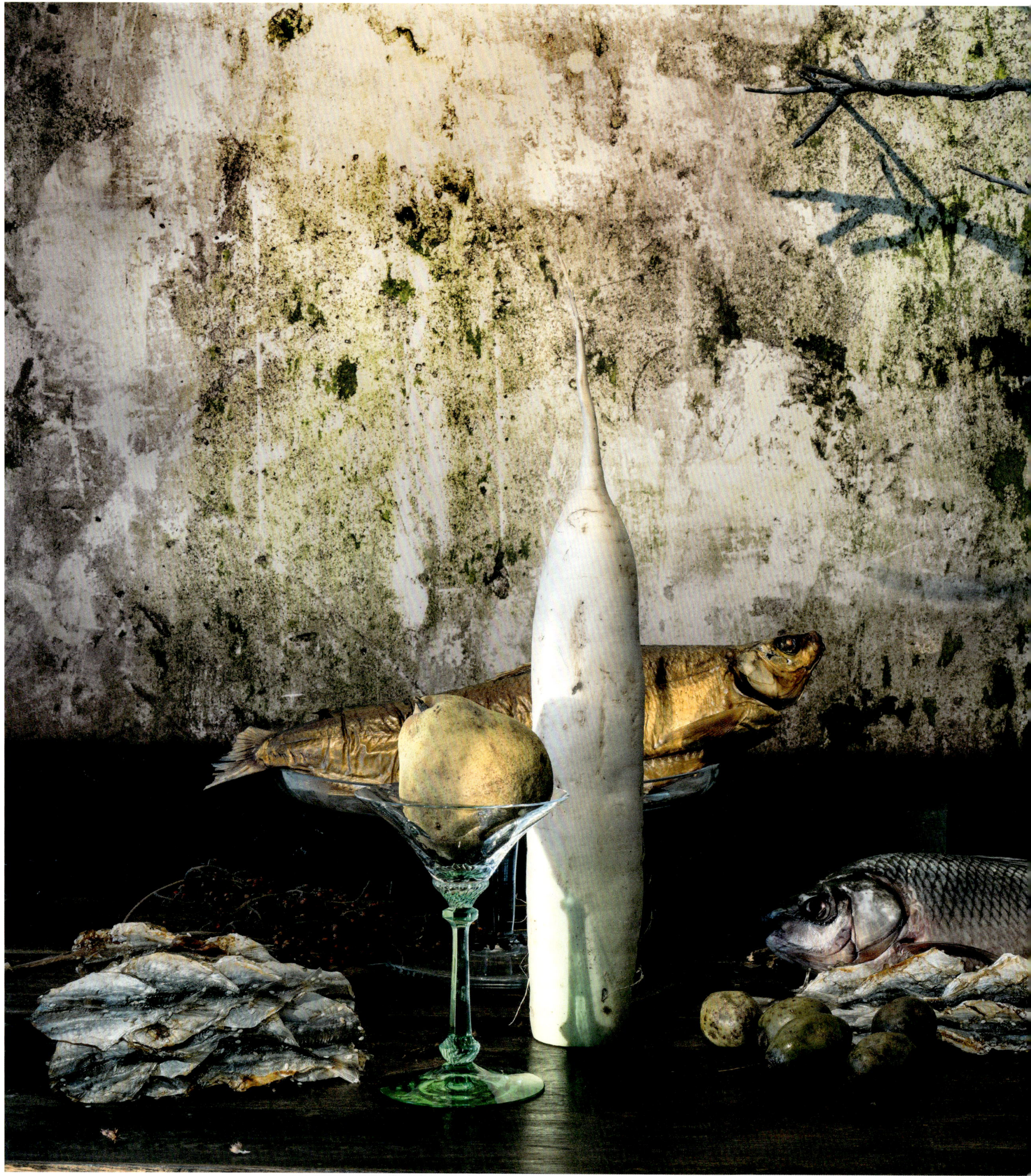

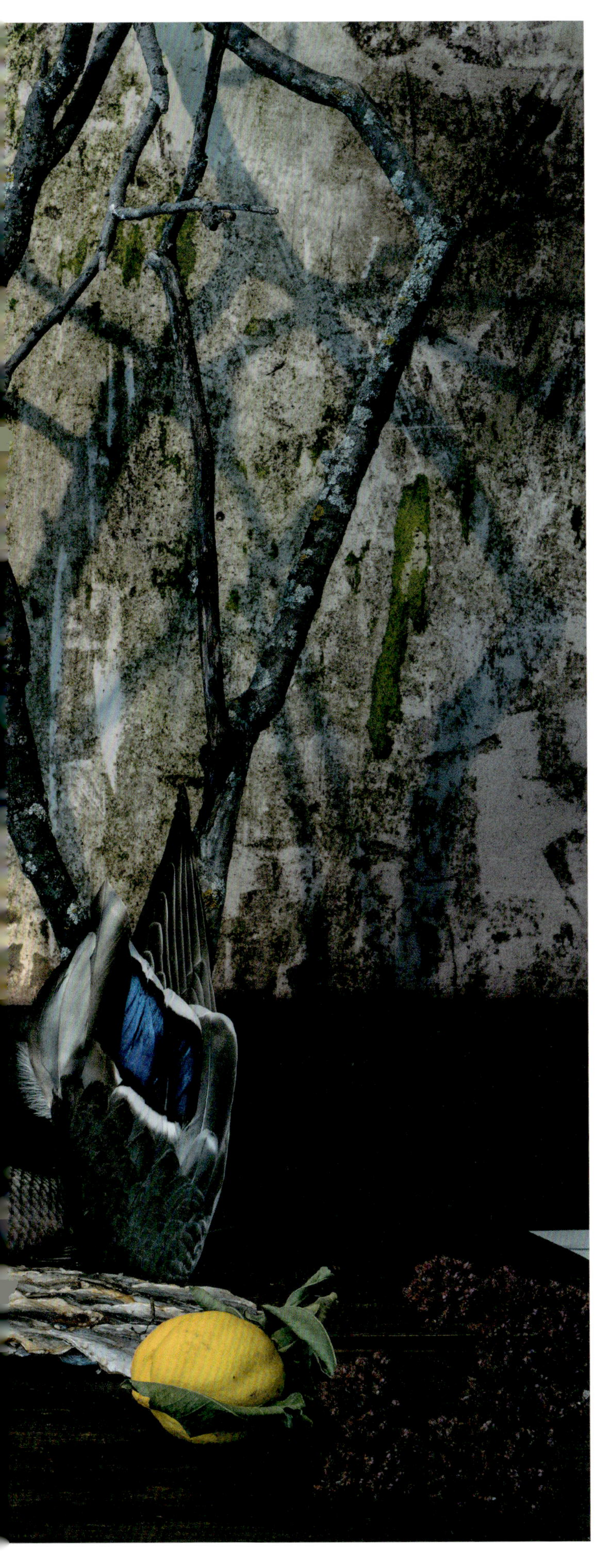

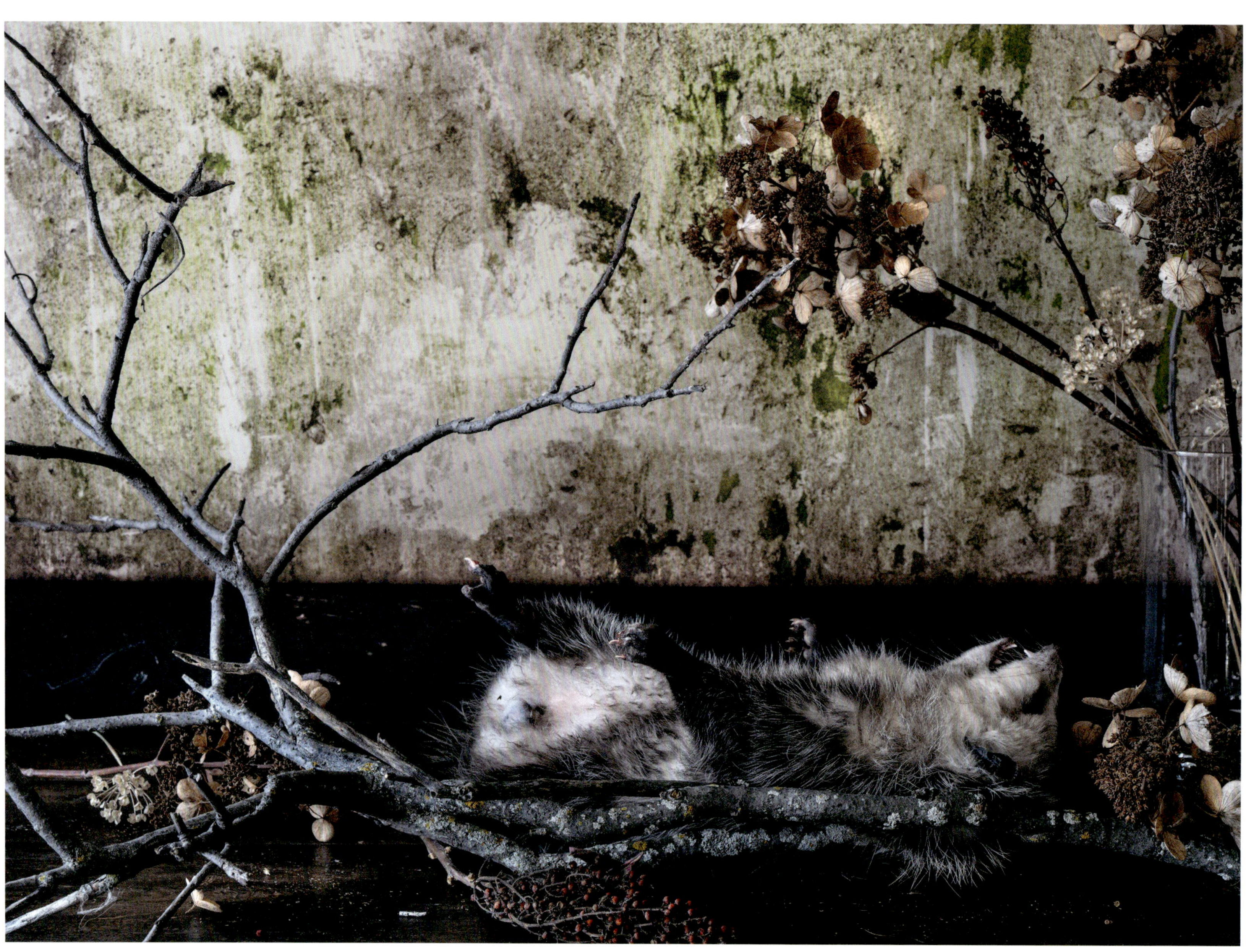

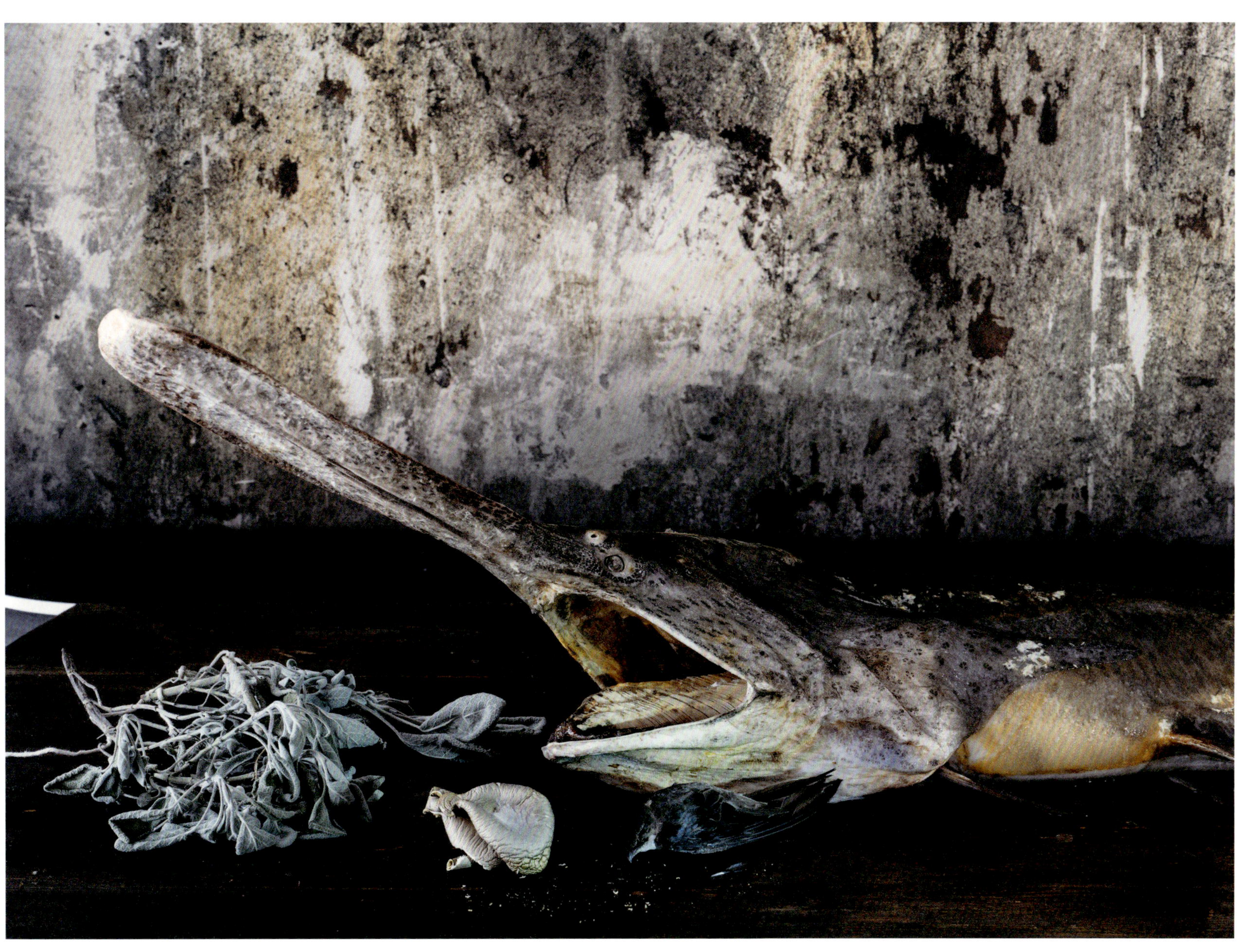

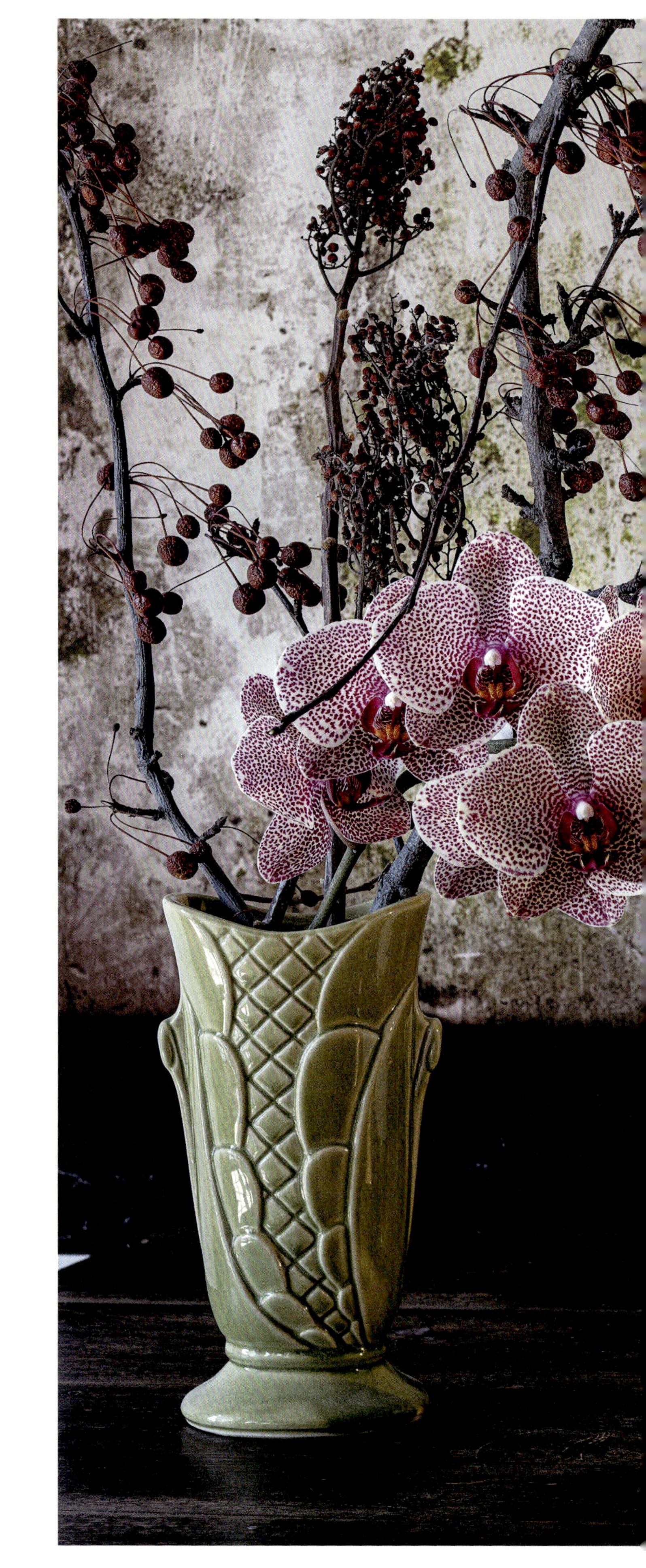

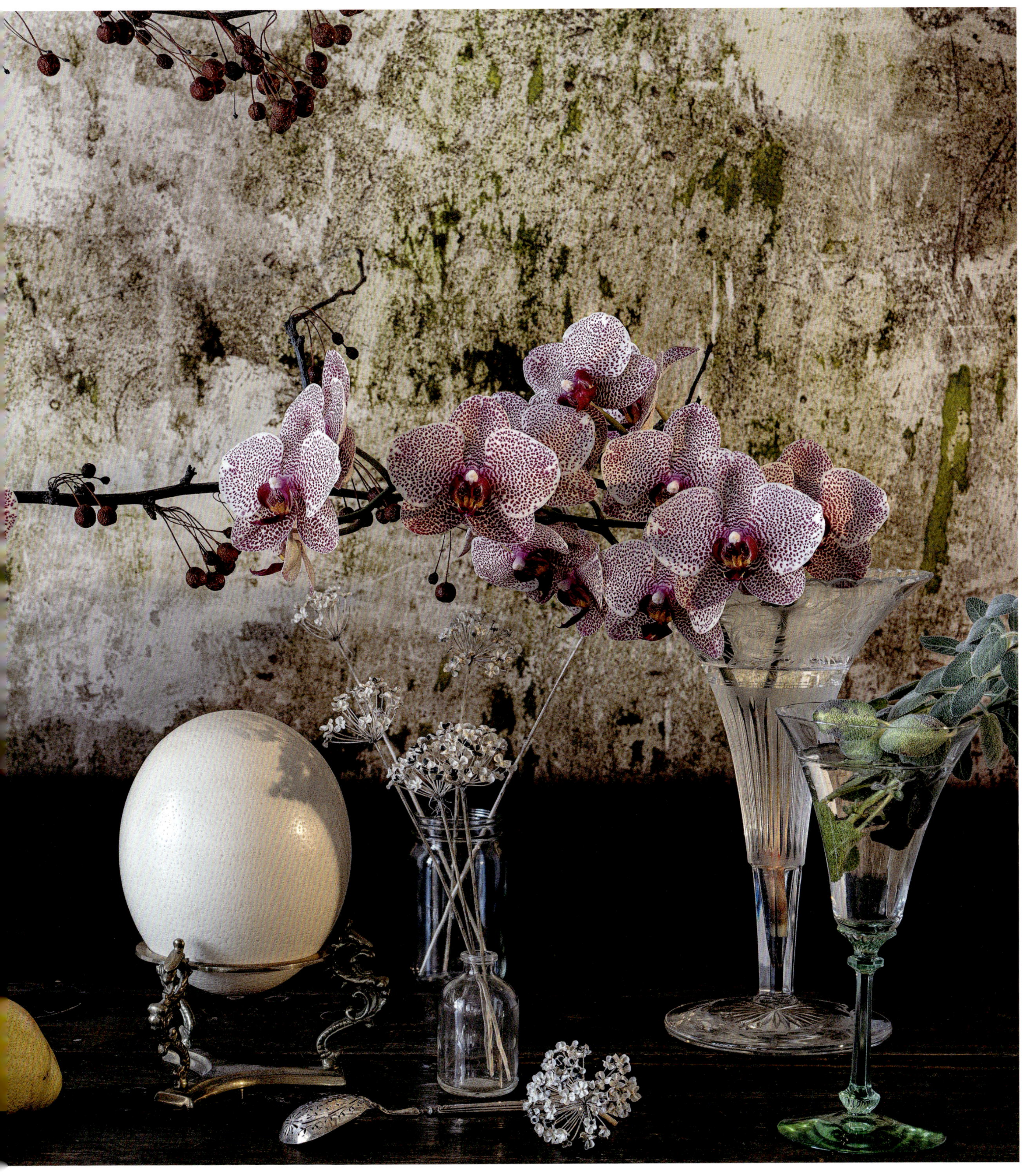

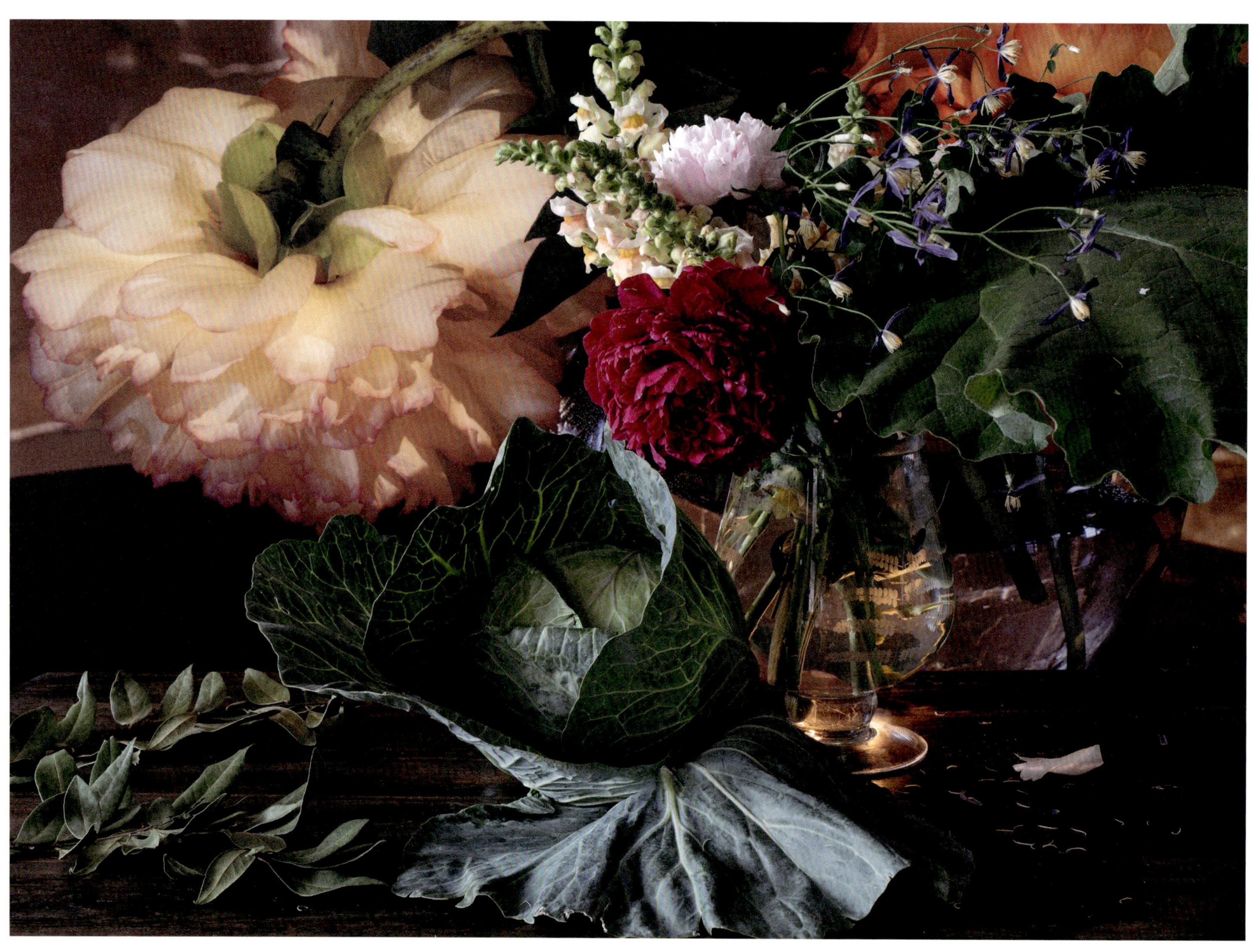

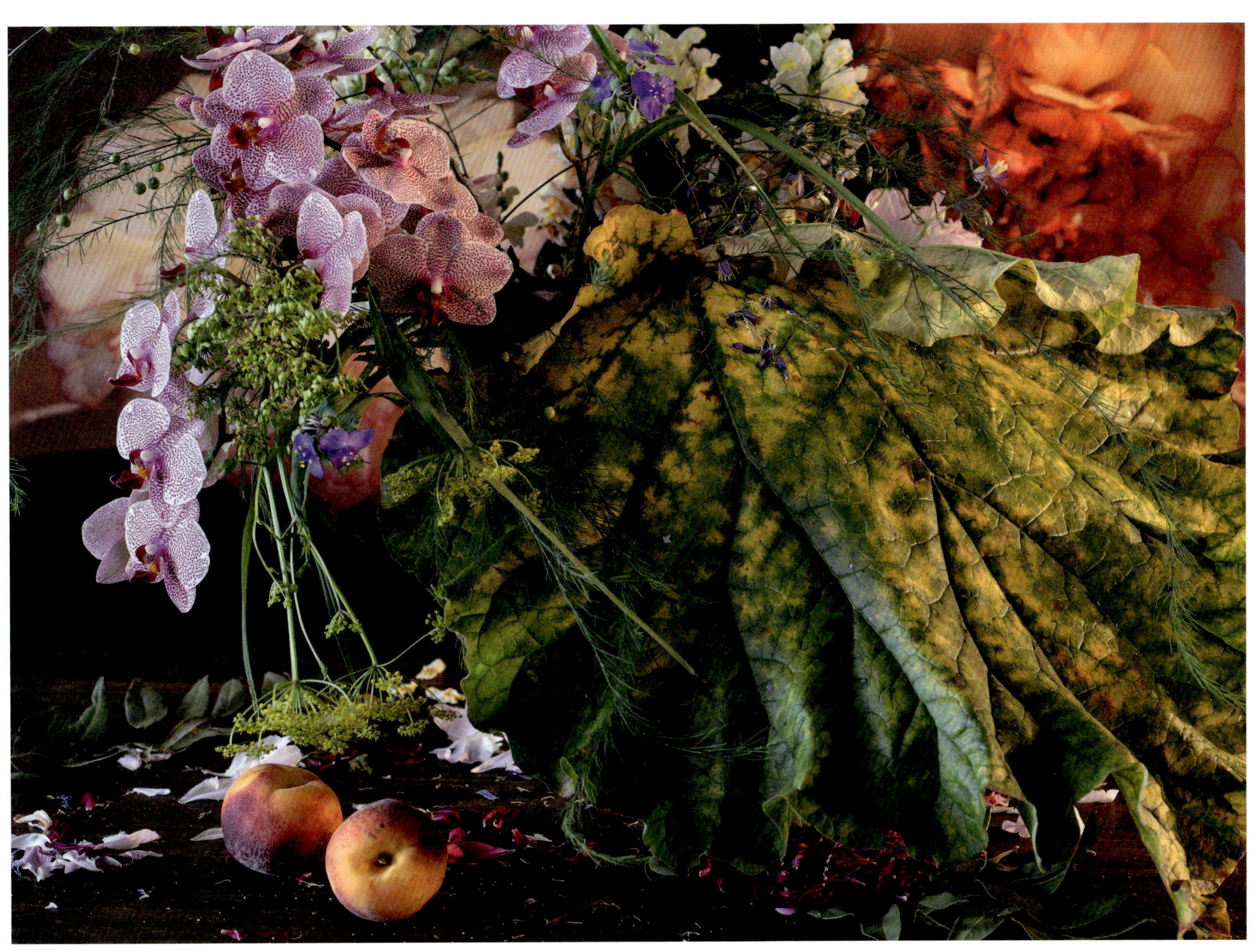

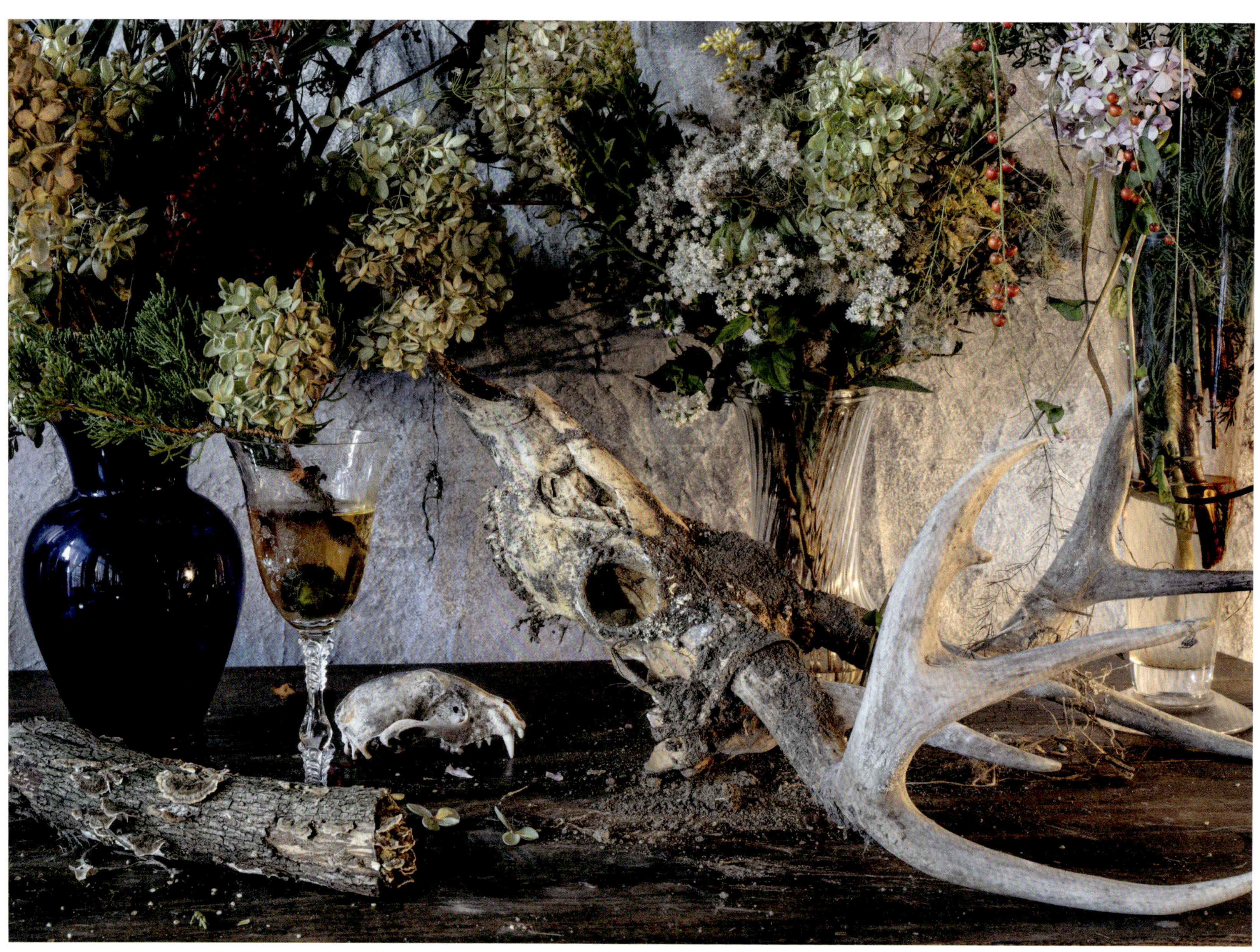

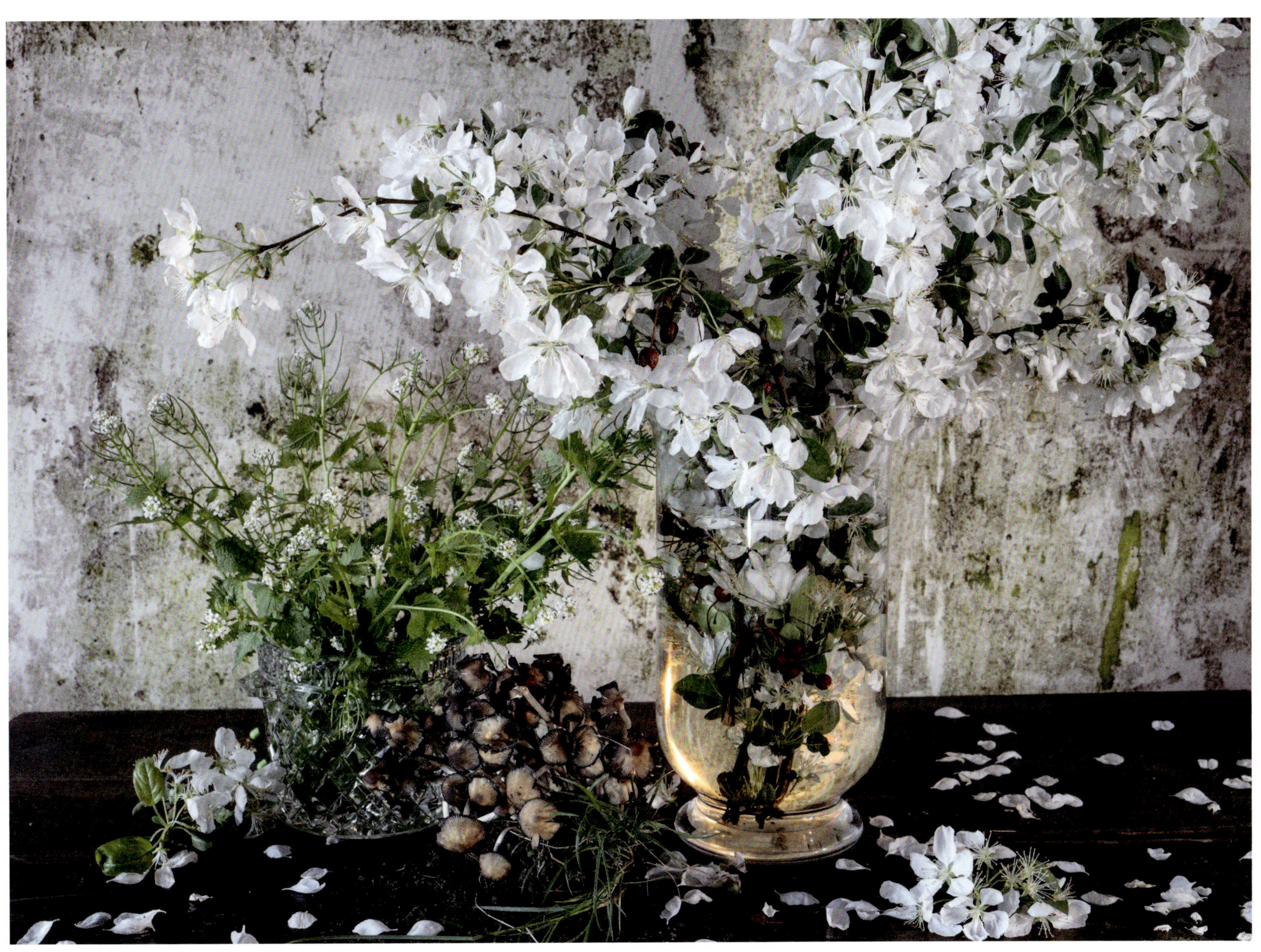

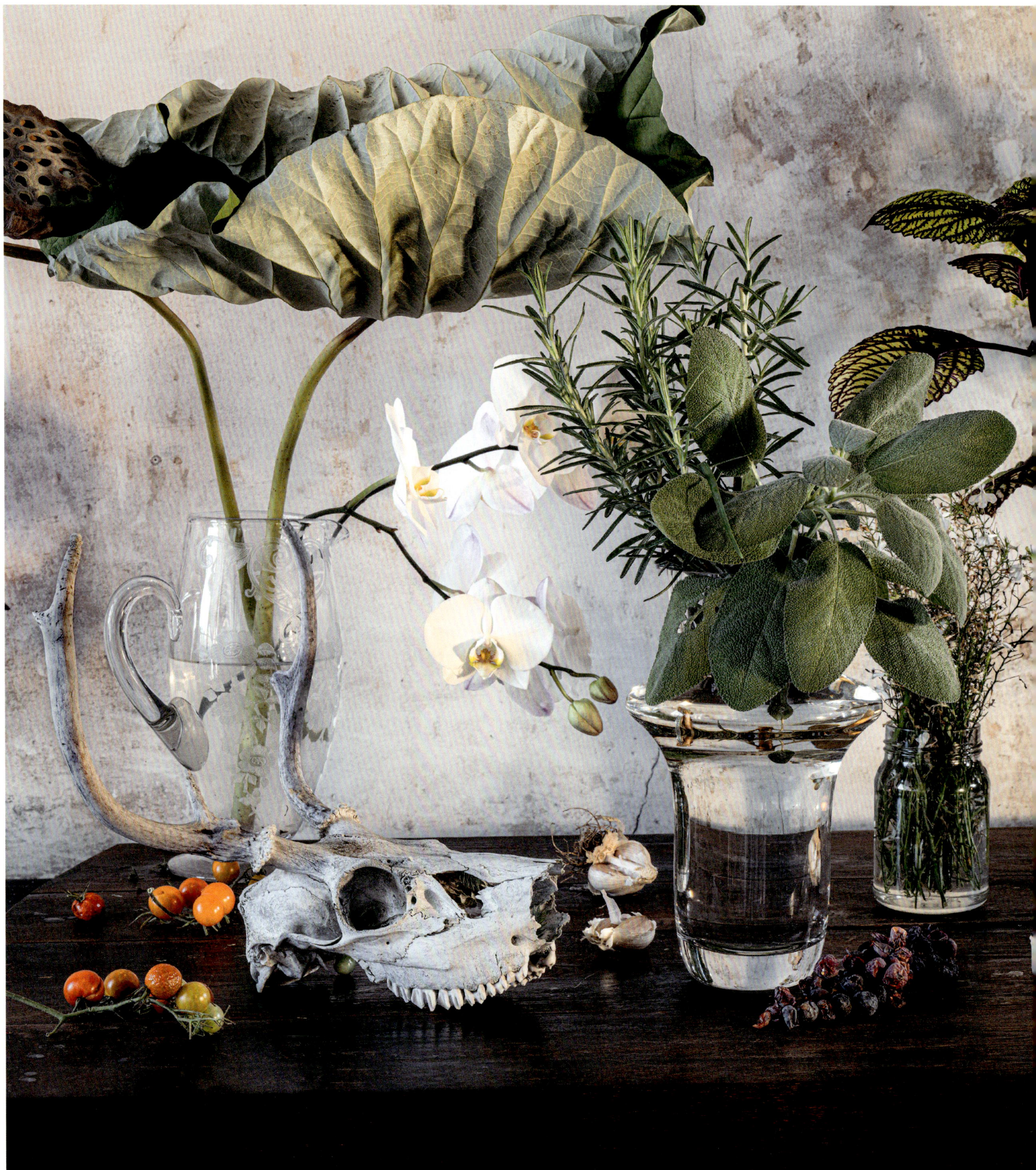

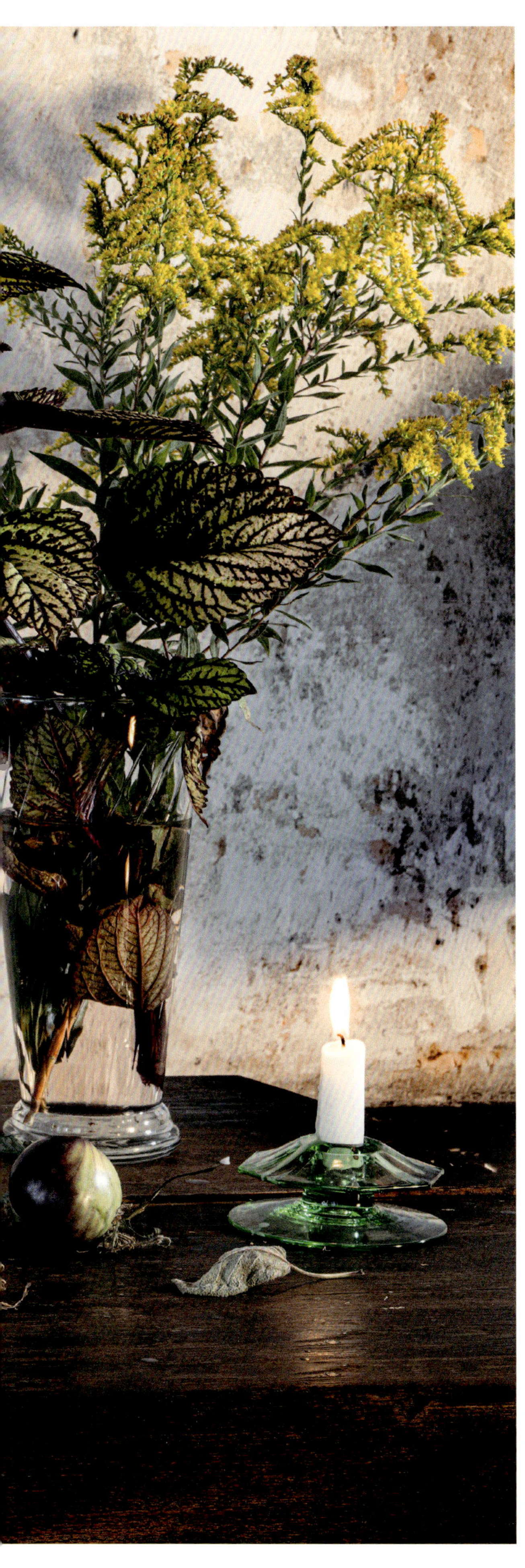

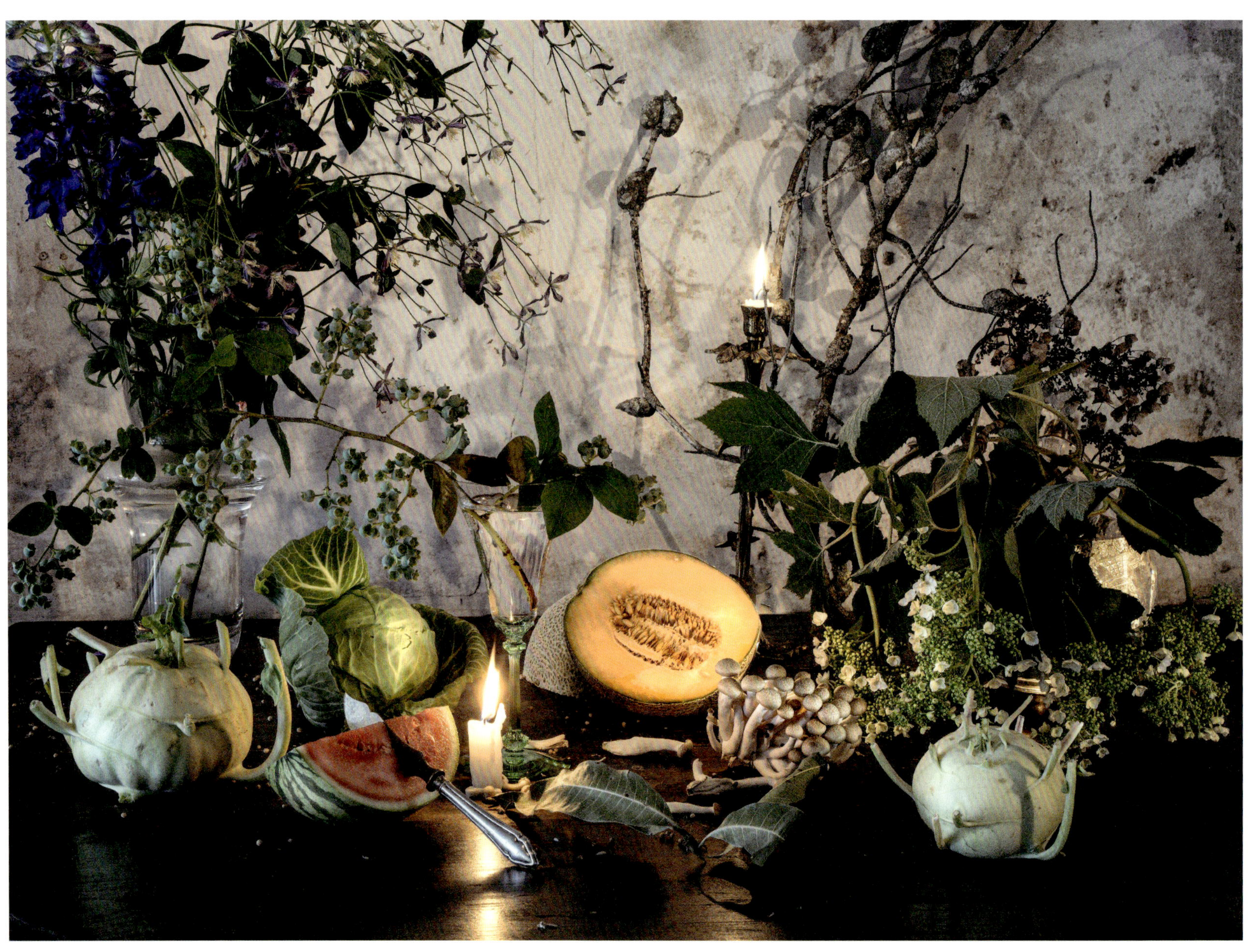

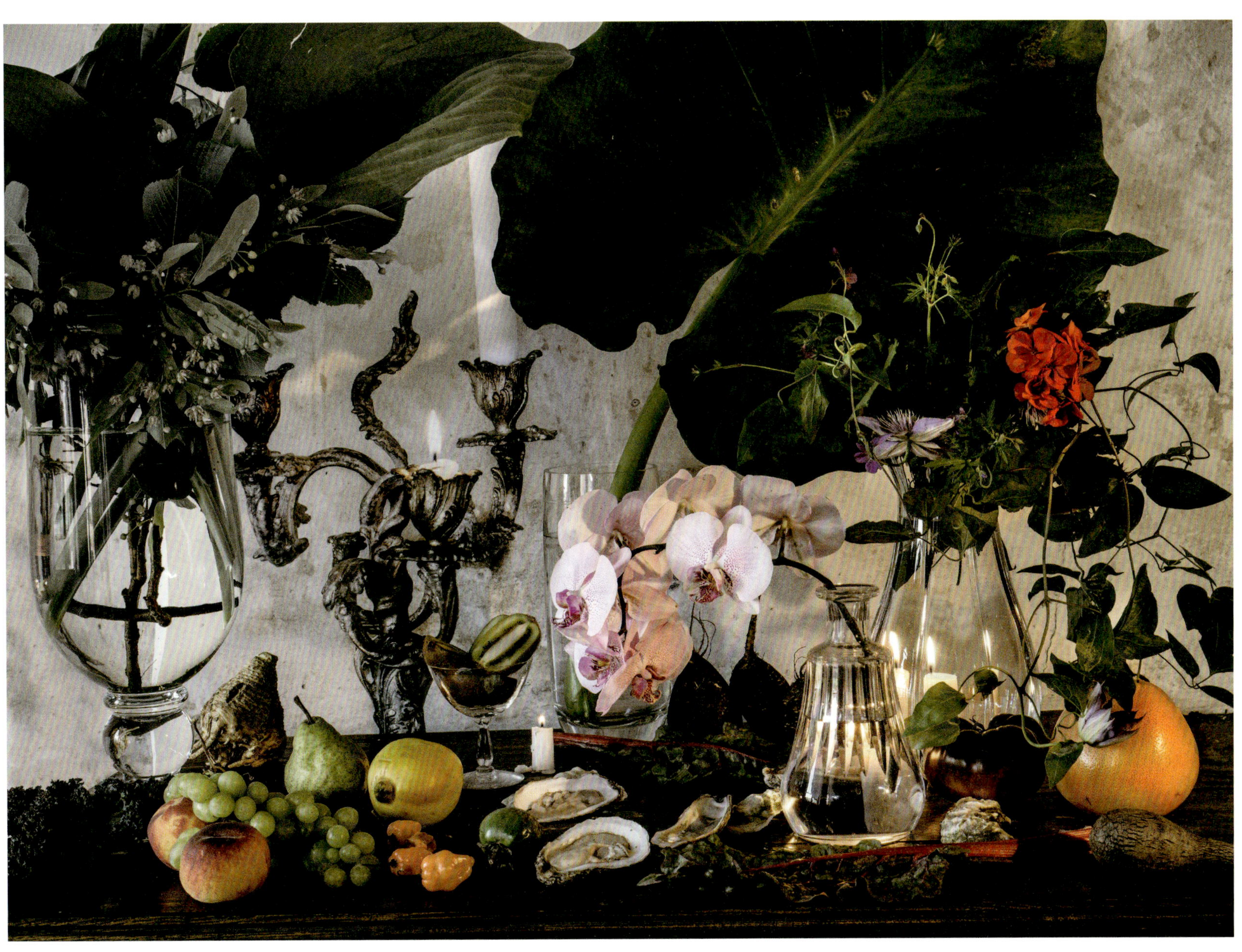

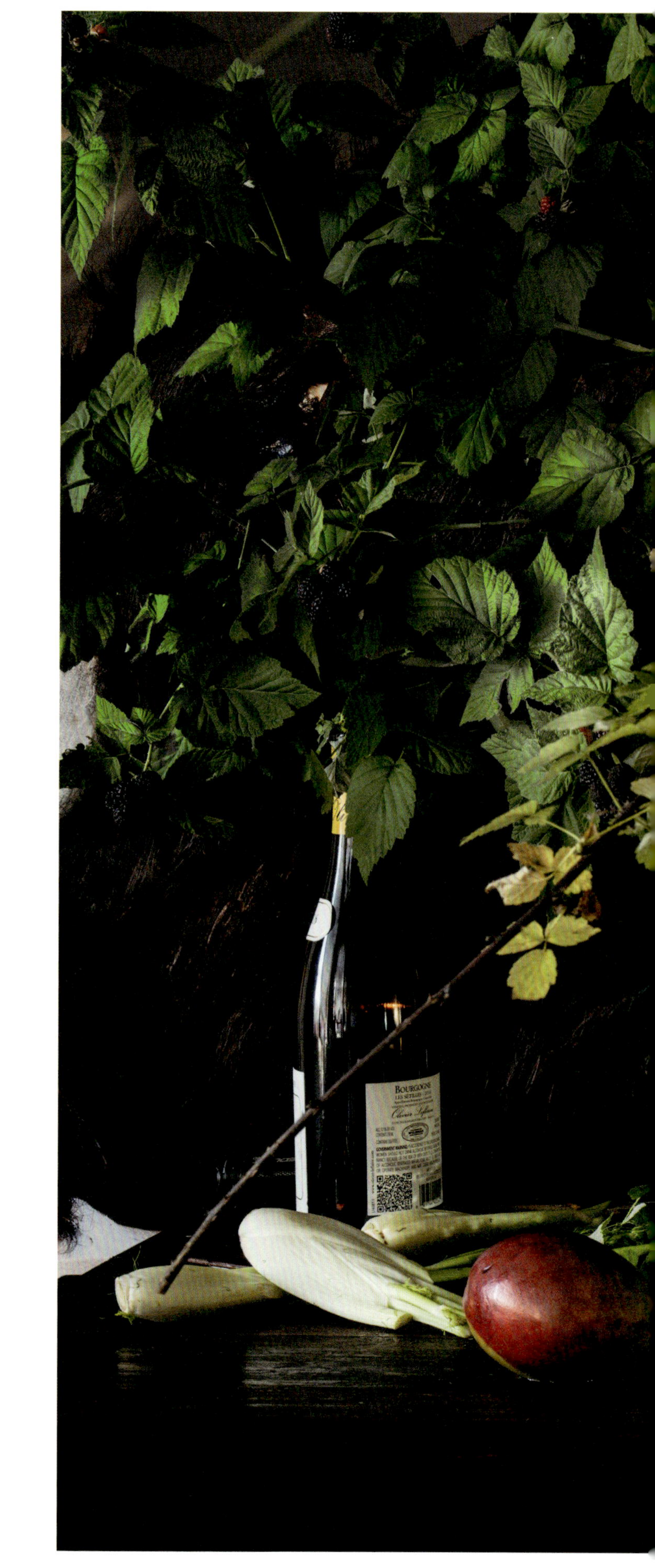
BOURGOGNE
LES SETILLES
GOVERNMENT WARNING

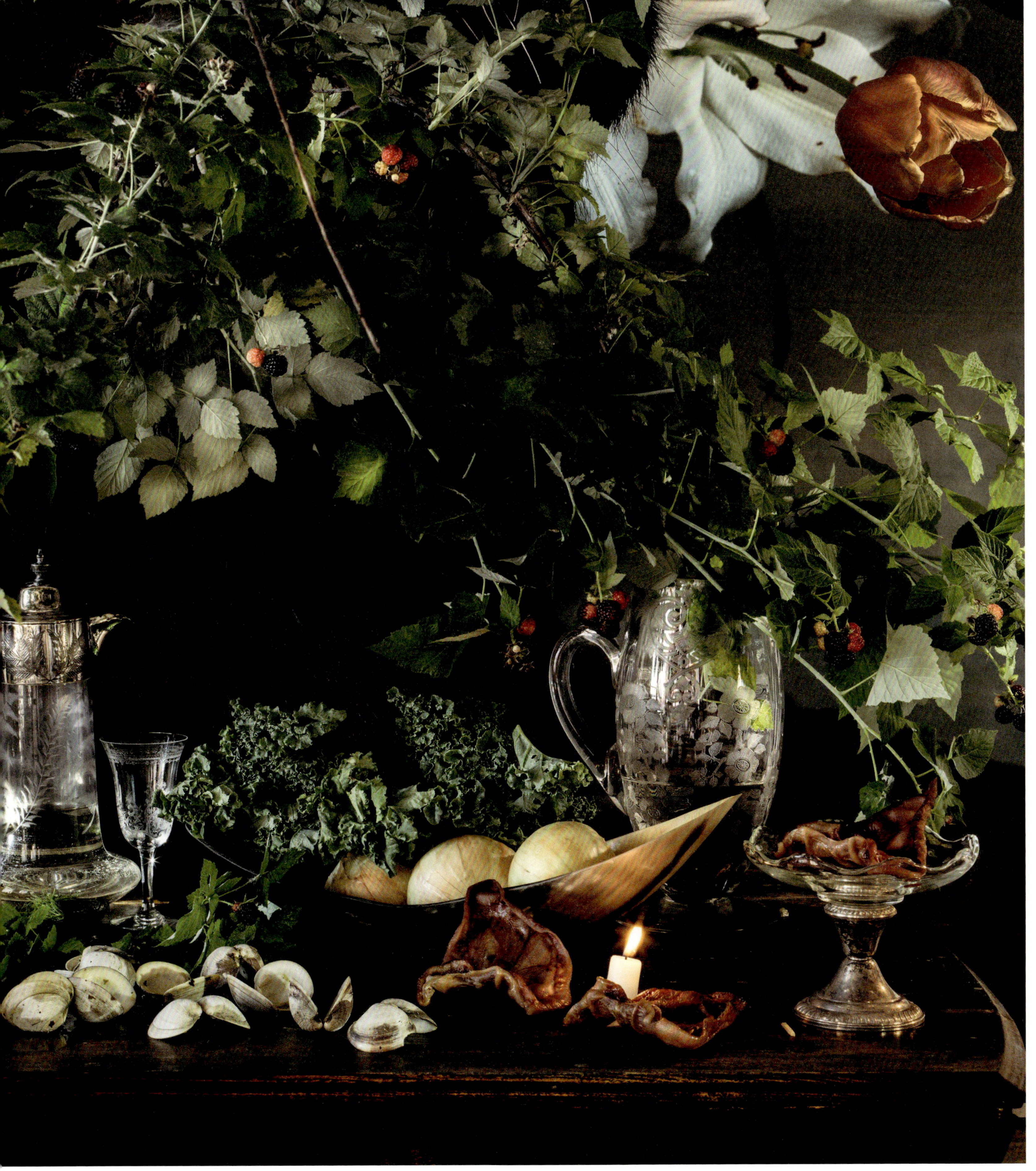

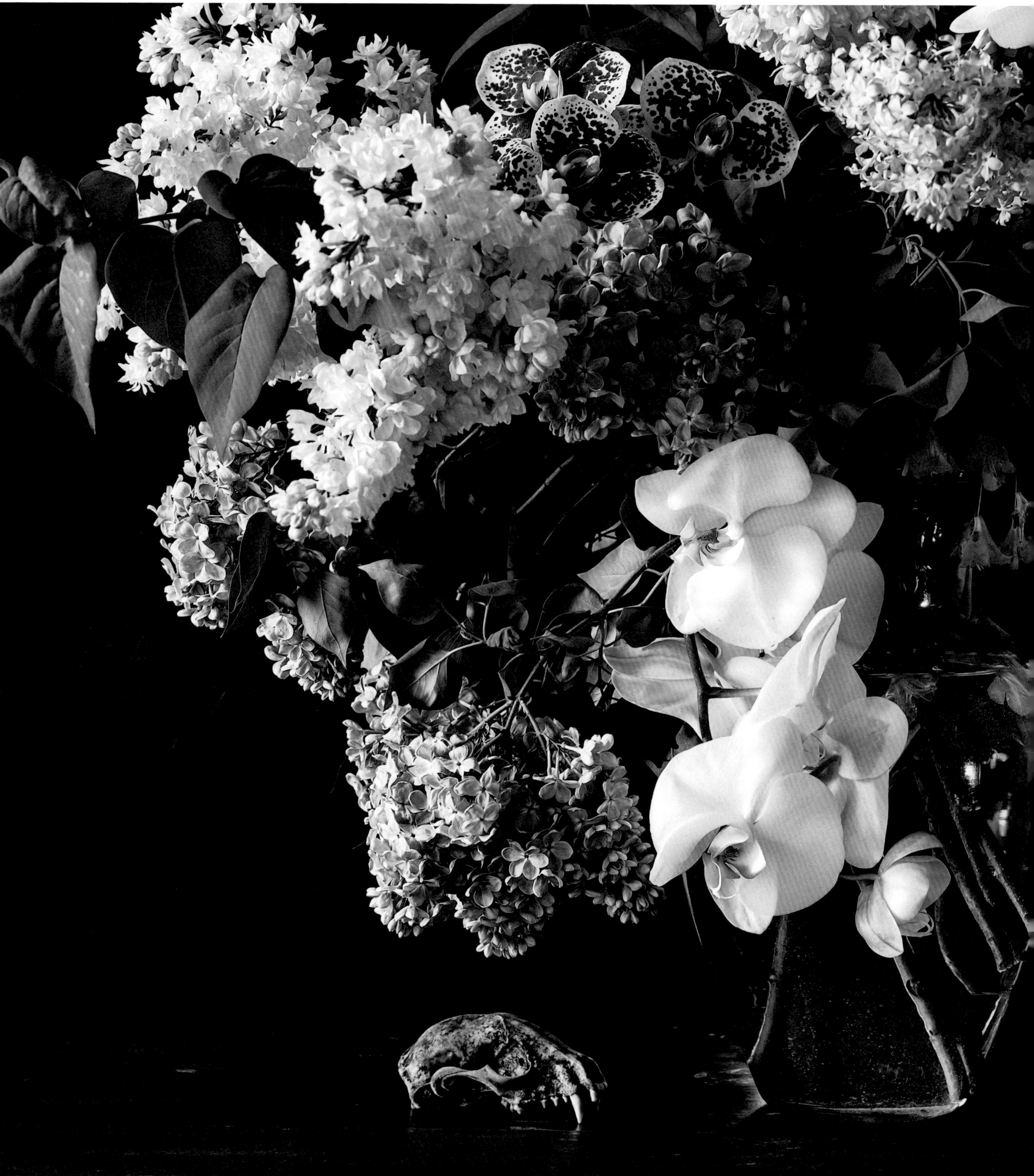

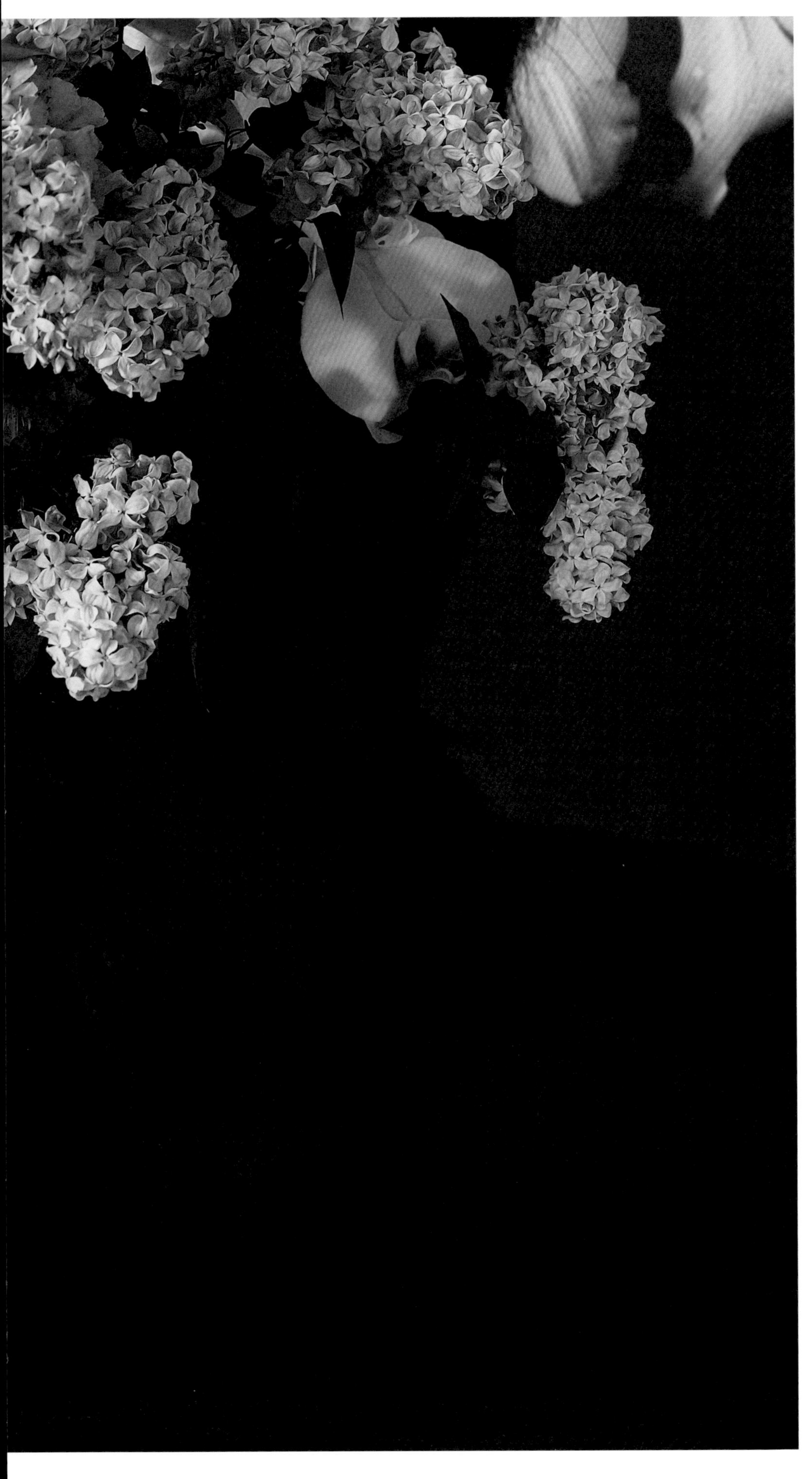

Sergio Fabio Berardini

BEIM ERSCHEINEN DES TODES. DER RITUS UND DIE KUNST

Seit Jahrhunderten denkt der Mensch über seine eigene Wesenhaftigkeit nach, im Unterschied zu Tieren und anderen nicht-menschlichen Lebewesen. So haben die Philosophen festgestellt, dass der Mensch das einzige Wesen ist, das die Fähigkeit zur Vernunft und Sprache besitzt. Ein Wesen, das in der Lage ist zu planen und zu handeln. Ein Sein, das aus Liebe lachen, lügen, Mitgefühl empfinden, dichten und weinen kann; ein Wesen, das sich ins Verhältnis zu göttlichen Wesenheiten stellt und noch viel mehr. Ein weiteres charakteristisches Merkmal des Menschen besteht darin, einerseits den Tod als schockierend zu betrachten und auf der anderen Seite diesen Schock durch kulturelle Handlungsweisen zu überwinden.
Der Tod wird vom Menschen immer „indirekt" erlebt. Da er die Erfahrung des eigenen Todes nicht machen kann, lernt er die Bedeutung des Sterbens durch das Sterben anderer. Dieses Ereignis verursacht Leid, vor allem, wenn es sich um den Tod eines von uns geliebten Menschen handelt: Man beweint den Verlust dieser Person. Dies geschieht gelegentlich auch bei einem Haustier, das uns über Jahre hinweg ein treuer Freund war. Der Tod wird als Leere empfunden. Der Tod des anderen ruft in uns Trauer und Melancholie hervor, ein Mitgefühl, das uns an die anderen bindet; so ist es möglich, über den Tod von unbekannten Personen oder beim Anblick eines toten Kätzchens bei einem Parkspaziergang zu weinen. Andererseits kann das Erscheinen des Todes in uns das beängstigende Bewusstsein erwecken, dass das Sterben eine „Möglichkeit" ist, die zu uns gehört, oder mit Martin Heidegger formuliert, dass der Tod unsere „ureigenste Möglichkeit" sei. In diesem Bewusstsein, dass unser Sein zum Tod bestimmt ist, darin beruht der Schrecken des Sterbens.
Der Tod wird als schockierendes Ereignis erlebt. Und deshalb verwenden die Menschen, im Unterschied zu anderen Lebewesen, nicht zufällig viel Energie darauf, sich vom Objekt, das der Leichnam darstellt, zu befreien. Der Körper der verstorbenen Person wird verborgen, aus der Welt der Lebenden entfernt – durch unterschiedlichste Rituale je nach Kulturkreis und Kulturzugehörigkeit. Der Leichnam wird beigesetzt, verbrannt, den Wassern übergeben, in tiefe Gräben geworfen oder, in Stücke zerteilt, den wilden Tieren zum Fraß vorgeworfen. Bei einigen Dichtern rufen die Toten die Assoziation von fallenden Blättern hervor. Die Anstrengung, die fallenden Blätter vor unseren Augen zu verbergen, kann man mit einem Heer von Straßenfegern vergleichen, die in einem nie enden wollenden Herbst verzweifelt versuchen, einen Waldboden sauber zu halten.
Obwohl die Bestattungsrituale den Leichnam beseitigen sollen, gehört die absichtliche Zurschaustellung desselben Leichnams

WHEN DEATH APPEARS. RITUALITY AND ART

Mankind has for centuries pondered his being with respect to those specific differences that distinguish our species from the other non-human animals. Thus philosophers have from time to time shown us that Man is, unlike every other animal, at the same time a being bestowed with reason and verbal language, a being that can plan and discuss, a being that can laugh, lie, and feel compassion, that can compose poetry and despair over love, a being that communicates with divine entities, and so on. In this sense, so far as such distinctions can totter and fall once subjected to criticism, we can also say that a typical characteristic of the human race is the ability it has to look at death and consider it a *scandal*, while, at the same time, it can win over this scandal through a *cultural operation*.
Man lives death indirectly; while he cannot experience his own death, he learns about it through the death of other persons. This event can be suffered as a loss, for instance when it is the death of a loved one; in this case one laments the demise of a person that one has loved or admired, but it could also be a pet that has been our friend for many a year. Such a death is lived as an emptiness, and so in this case we call it mourning. Someone's death can also inspire a sense of sadness, of melancholy, so that we perceive empathy, which ties us to other humans: one can cry for the death of a stranger or for the sight of a dead kitten stumbled upon during a walk in the park. At the same time, the summoning of death can reawaken in our inner selves the anxious knowledge that our own death is a possibility, or, in Martin Heidegger's words, "one's ownmost potentiality-for-being." The loss, the mourning, the frailty on whose foundation the sympathetic knots that tie us to the outside world are based, the knowledge that our being's fate is death: this is what the scandal of dying is based on (and probably on other things too).
Death is experienced as a scandal. So it does not come as a surprise that mankind, unlike other species, spends so much effort in getting rid of that scandalous object, the corpse. The dead person's body is hidden, put out of sight, distanced from the world of the living – every culture has developed its own rituals to do such a thing. The corpse is buried, burned, slipped into water, thrown into deep ravines, cut into pieces and fed to voracious animals, and so on. If a dead person may have evoked, in some poetical minds, the image of fallen leaves, then the activity of concealing these leaves must be perceived as that of an army of gardeners who, despairing in the face of a never-ending autumn, try to keep the forest floor clean.
At the same time, while funerary rituals endeavor to eliminate the corpse, they also consist in its deliberate exposition – an

zum Ritual dazu. Diese Zurschaustellung ist meist jedoch zeitlich begrenzt. Nur in Ausnahmefällen ist er auf Dauer angelegt, beispielsweise bei einbalsamierten Leichnamen in Mausoleen und Heiligtümern. Die Beseitigung eines Leichnams findet häufig im Rahmen von Zeremonien statt, die einer Zurschaustellung entsprechen, um den Leichnam öffentlich sichtbar zu machen. In dieser inneren Dialektik, die das Beseitigen mit der Zurschaustellung verbindet, können die Bestattungsrituale als ein „zweiter Tod" gesehen werden. Durch diese Rituale wird der Tote aus dem Sichtfeld der Lebenden genommen. Die Lebenden, die darauf bestehen, dem Akt der Beseitigung des Toten beizuwohnen, erleben einen zweiten Tod. Eine Funktion der Bestattungsrituale besteht also darin, sich dem Schrecken des Todes zu stellen und ihn mit Hilfe solcher Rituale zu überwinden. Um dieses Konzept zu verstehen, müssen wir begreifen, worin der Schrecken des Todes begründet ist. Das Schockierende ist nicht so sehr, dass der Tod sich als Leichnam zeigt oder in den körperlichen Details des Todes, etwa gewissen Farben und Gerüchen, sondern vielmehr das Verhältnis des Menschen zum Tod an sich. Was ist nun seine Bedeutung? Die Sinnlosigkeit! In der Tat zeigt sich das Schockierende in dem Moment, in dem sich der Tod in seiner gesamten Sinnlosigkeit offenbart. Mit anderen Worten, der Mensch ist schockiert von der Sinnlosigkeit des Todes – einer Sinnlosigkeit, die das Leben infizieren kann (der „Krankheit zum Tode" mit den Worten von Søren Kierkegaard). Es ist diese Sinnlosigkeit, die die Lebenden ärgert, und sie davon überzeugt, dass das Leben selbst keinen Sinn hat.
Kommen wir nun zu der Funktion der Totenrituale; sie dienen dazu, dieses schreckenerregende Objekt, das der Leichnam darstellt, zu beseitigen – weiterhin bewirkt eine Zurschaustellung des Leichnams eine Zurschaustellung des Todes im Allgemeinen. Der Schrecken kann im Ritual durch die Zurschaustellung und Beseitigung des Leichnams überwunden werden. Bei den Bestattungsritualen werden die Lebenden, die als Zuschauer der Demonstration des Todes beiwohnen, vom Tode selbst abgelenkt. Dem Leichnam wird in diesem Zusammenhang eine bestimmte Rolle zugedacht: Er ist nun nicht mehr abstoßend, sondern wird bühnenreif, nimmt also eine herausragende Position auf der Bühne ein. Durch diese ritualisierte Zurschaustellung wird der Leichnam seiner sinnlosen, ja inakzeptablen Präsenz entzogen und auf eine kulturelle Ebene gehoben. Das Ritual hat somit die Aufgabe, den toten Körper in seiner schamlosen Nacktheit mit Bedeutung zu bekleiden. Das Gewand, das den Leichnam in dieser Situation der Zurschaustellung bedeckt – eine Bekleidung im bildlichen, nicht im wörtlichen Sinn –, verwandelt den Körper des Verstorbenen in einen Körper, der den Lebenden gezeigt werden kann – einen „in Szene" gesetzten Körper. Durch diesen kulturellen Akt wird der Schock überwunden, und das Sterben wie der Tod werden in das Leben der Lebenden integriert, trotz all des Schmerzes. Dem natürlichen Tod folgt

exposition that can be much prolonged in time (as in the case of those embalmed bodies shown in mausoleums or shrines), but which usually is of a limited nature, because these rituals are studied to precede and prepare for the hiding of the body. This apparent paradox is justified by the fact that the act of removing requires the removed object, which, to be removed, has to manifest itself. The corpse's removal is therefore enacted through ceremonies that tend to exhibit the body and make it public. Within this dialectic, which binds hiding to showing, we can interpret funerary rituals as a kind of second death, which allows the deceased to be removed from the sight of the living. It is the living who insist, in this manner, in seeing their own second death in the act of removing the dead.
The function of a funerary ritual is to challenge and beat the scandal of death. To understand this we have to consider what constitutes the scandal of death. It isn't the object in which death reveals itself (the corpse) that is scandalous, nor are its physical characteristics (certain colors, smells, etc.) scandalous. The scandal lies within man's relationship with death, the meaning that death has in the mind of man. What form does this meaning have? The loss of meaning. The scandal lies in the fact that death is something devoid of sense. In other words, man is scandalized by the senselessness of death – a senselessness that can infect life with the same illness (*The Sickness Unto Death,* as Søren Kierkegaard put it); it is this lack of meaning that annoys the living, convincing them that life itself has no meaning. But what is the point of these funerary rituals? We have said that they are in place to get rid of that foul object, the corpse; we have also said that that riddance needs the exhibition of the same, i.e. an exhibition of death. We therefore win over the scandal through the "exhibition-riddance" of the corpse – of the earthly remains of the person lost to death. During the funerary rituals the living, who are spectators, even though they are viewing the manifestation of death, are at the same time distracted by death, or rather: they are distracted by the senselessness of the crudity of death. The ritual distracts the spectators from the mere *fait accompli*, the obscenity of the corpse. This object is given an order of meaning: it is no longer obscene (abominable, dirty, and therefore rightly excluded from the "scenery"), but rather it becomes "scenic," it has the privilege to occupy the scene: the center stage belongs to it.
As we have said, the corpse's obscenity necessitates its removal. The corpse is taken away from the sight of the living, but this happens through a ritual that implies its exhibition. Due to this ritualized exhibition, the corpse is torn away from its meaningless (and unacceptable and repelling) presence and translated into a cultural plane. The ritual's task is therefore to clothe that corpse with meaning, which would otherwise be senseless, if left naked. The shroud with which the corpse is covered (a figurative, not literal shroud) makes the corpse a decent one for viewing by those

ein kulturell gestalteter Tod, der vom Menschen bestimmt wird. Dieser macht sich zum „Bevollmächtigten des Todes“ (Ernesto de Martino), indem er die Regie des Sternes übernimmt – er entwickelt einen Tod auf kultureller Ebene; ein Sterben, das so in den menschlichen Lebenslauf eingeschlossen werden kann.

Die fotografischen Kompositionen von Vera Mercer scheinen, auch wenn sie nicht auf eine reine Form der Bestattungsrituale zurückgeführt werden können, trotz allem die eigentliche Funktion dieser Rituale zu übernehmen. Durch diese „in Licht gemeißelten Grabmonumente“ (Tatiana Richilmini) nehmen wir an einer Zurschaustellung des Todes teil, welche die Schamlosigkeit des Leichnams durch seine sorgfältige und gewissenhafte Inszenierung begrenzt. Die hier zur Schau gestellten Körper befinden sich in einer Art „Todestheater“, in dem der Tod kein Problem darstellt. Die in den Fotografien von Mercer dargestellten Überreste werden „entsterblicht“: Sie werden wieder in das Theater des Lebens aufgenommen, nachdem sie davon ausgeschlossen wurden. In diesem Sinne kann man von einer „toten Natur“ sprechen, einem „Stillleben“.

Es ist kein Element dem Zufall überlassen, so wie es bei den feierlichsten Ritualen üblich ist, wo das menschliche Handeln alles durchdringt. Schatten und Glanz des Lichtes, Kälte und Wärme, die pflanzlichen und tierischen Körper – die feinen, noch weichen Federkleider, dem Blick offenbart, wie reife Granatäpfel – alle einzelnen Teile bilden die Bühne, auf der die Gegenwart des niedergelegten und ausgestellten Leichnams ohne Scham möglich wird. Eine szenografische Präsenz, ein zentraler Anziehungspunkt: Der Blick des Betrachters wird von dem Stillleben in den Bann gezogen, auch wenn das Auge nur für kurze Momente abschweift, um sich am chromatischen und semantischen Spektakel zu erfreuen. Ein Spektakel, das Ausdruck einer menschlichen Entscheidung ist, d.h. eine ganz und gar menschliche Komposition, der es gelingt, den Tod auszutreiben.

So drückt sich hier, ebenso wie bei anderen Totenritualen, der Widerstand des Lebens gegenüber dem Tod aus; ein Sein, das noch am Leben ist und sich bemüht, dem Tod eine Bedeutung beizumessen. Eine kulturelle Anstrengung, deren Ziel es ist, dem Tod einen Sinn zu geben – seiner Sinnlosigkeit, dem Schrecken, seiner semantischen Obszönität, verursacht durch seinen Mangel an Bedeutung. In den Bestattungsritualen drückt sich dieser Widerstand im Rückgriff auf Symbole und Erzählungen religiöser Art aus, hier hingegen wird eine rein ästhetische Form verwendet, eine sorgfältige Suche nach dem „schönen Ausdruck“ einer Ordnung, einer Anmut.

Die tote Natur wird hier durch menschliches Handeln am Leben erhalten, eine Intervention, die auf einem überaus menschlichen Prinzip beruht: Der Suche der Sinnhaftigkeit, der Suche nach einem Sinn, der sich nicht nur in Worten und der Wortgewandtheit von Diskursen ausdrückt, sondern auch in Taten (Ritualen) und Bildern (Kunst).

who live – a "theatrical" corpse. Thanks to a cultural act, the scandal is therefore vanquished, and dying becomes integrated into the life of those who live as something un-obscene, however painful it may be.

The function of the funerary ritual is to procure the corpse a "second death." Natural death, occurring against human will (it is this impotence in the face of death that makes mankind a mortal being) is followed by cultural death: a death that is chosen by man, that responds to human will and human control, the point of which is to "decease" death itself. Man himself becomes the "death getter" (Ernesto de Martino) directing death – processing death according to culture – and in this manner allowing death to be included within the course of human life.

Vera Mercer's photographic compositions, though not strictly definable as a funerary ritual, seem, however, to assume the function of these rituals. Even in these "light sculpted funerary monuments" (Tatiana Richilmini) we find an exhibition of death that limits the corpse's obscenity, thanks to an accurate and scrupulous staging. The bodies are exhibited as a kind of "mortal theater" in which death is no longer a problem. The remains shown in Mercer's photographs are "un-deaded": they have been reintroduced into life's theater after being mortally excluded. Thus we can talk of *natura morta,* which is "still life."

No element has been left to chance, in the same way that characterizes the most solemn of rituals, making human action wholly present. Shades and brightnesses, coldness and heat, vegetable remains and animals – the delicate, still downy, feathering, spread out to be seen like ripe pomegranates – every part staged so as not to make the exhibited body obscene. A scenic presence that becomes a gravitational center: the spectator cannot but be captivated by it, even though the eye will sometimes wander, if only for brief moments, so as to feast on the chromatic and semantic spectacle that supports it. A spectacle that is the expression of human choice, i.e. a wholly human composition, which succeeds in exorcising death.

In this manner, as in the funerary rituals, life's resistance to death expresses itself. That being "still alive," that fulfills itself in a cultural resistance whose purpose it is to give meaning to death – pent on taking away from death its senselessness, its scandal, its semantic obscenity caused by a lack of meaning. While this resistance expresses itself in funerary rituals through the use of religious symbologies and narratives, here we behold a purely aesthetic form, through the scrupulous research of a "beautiful countenance" (of order, of grace). The *natura morta* (dead nature) is here kept alive (still life) thanks to human intention and intervention – thanks to that exquisitely human principle that urges the search for a meaning, a meaning that expresses itself not only through words and the verbosity of discourse, but also thanks to deeds (ritual) and images (art)

PLATINUM PRINTS

PARIS AND OMAHA, 2018 – 2021

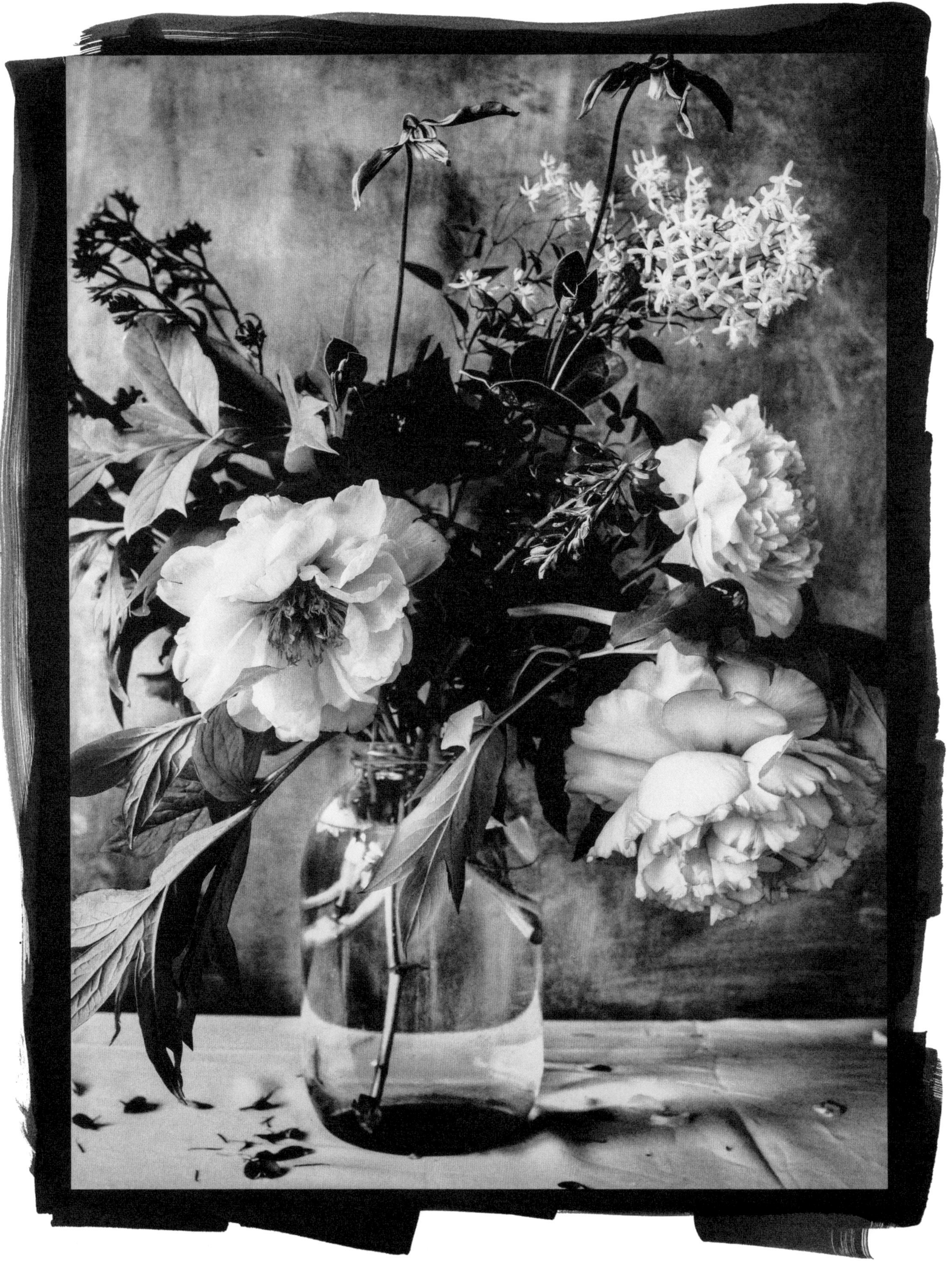

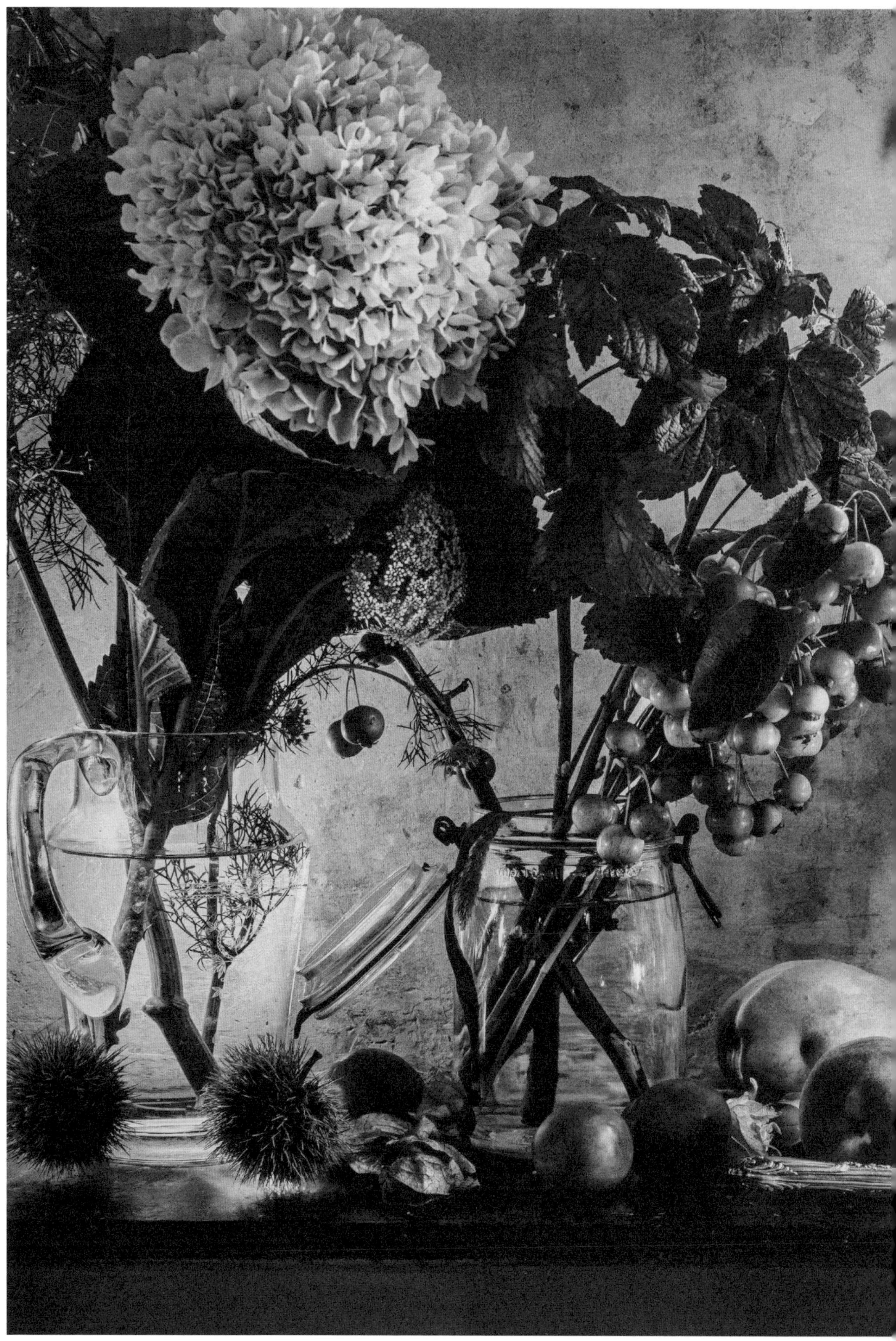

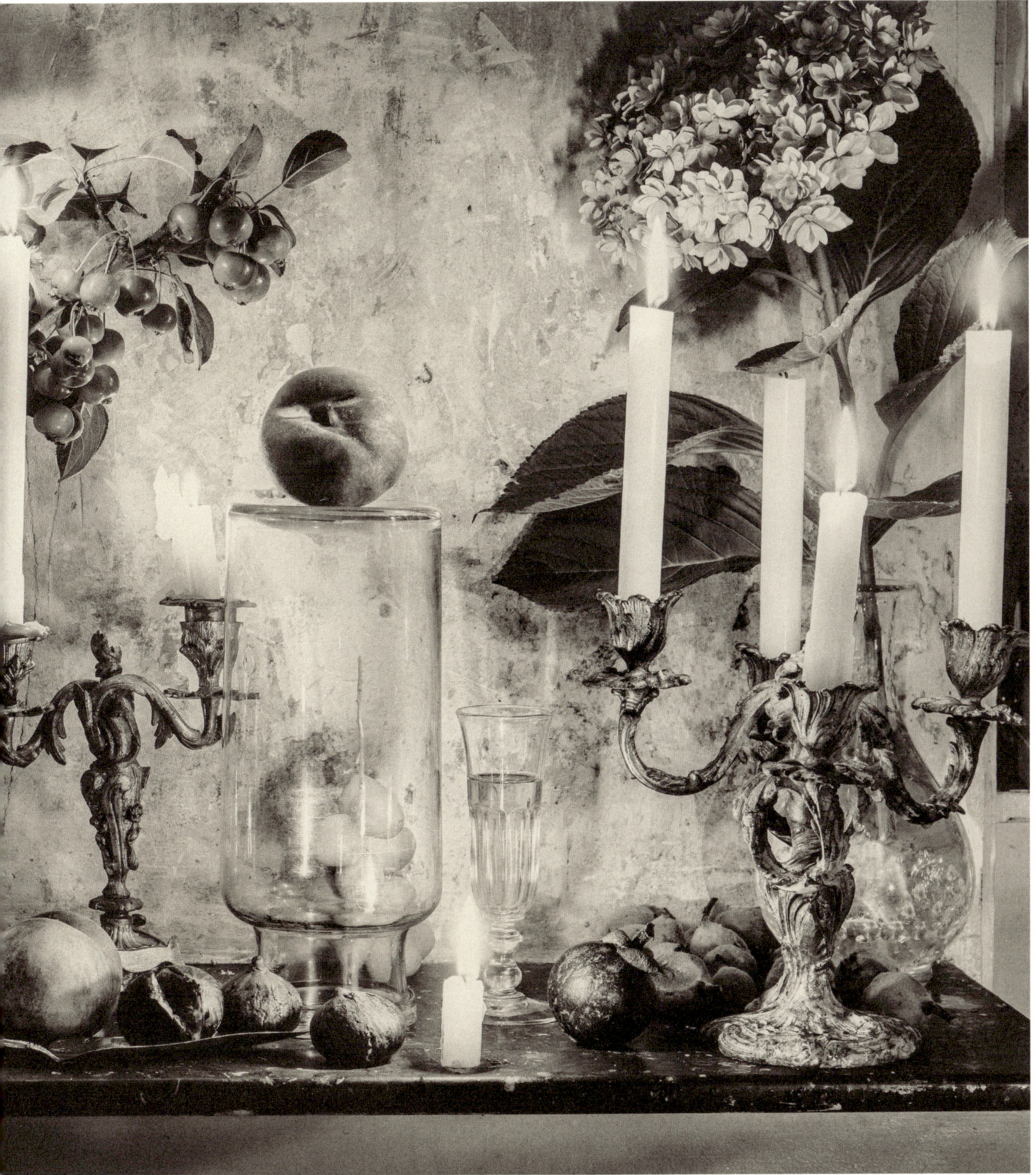

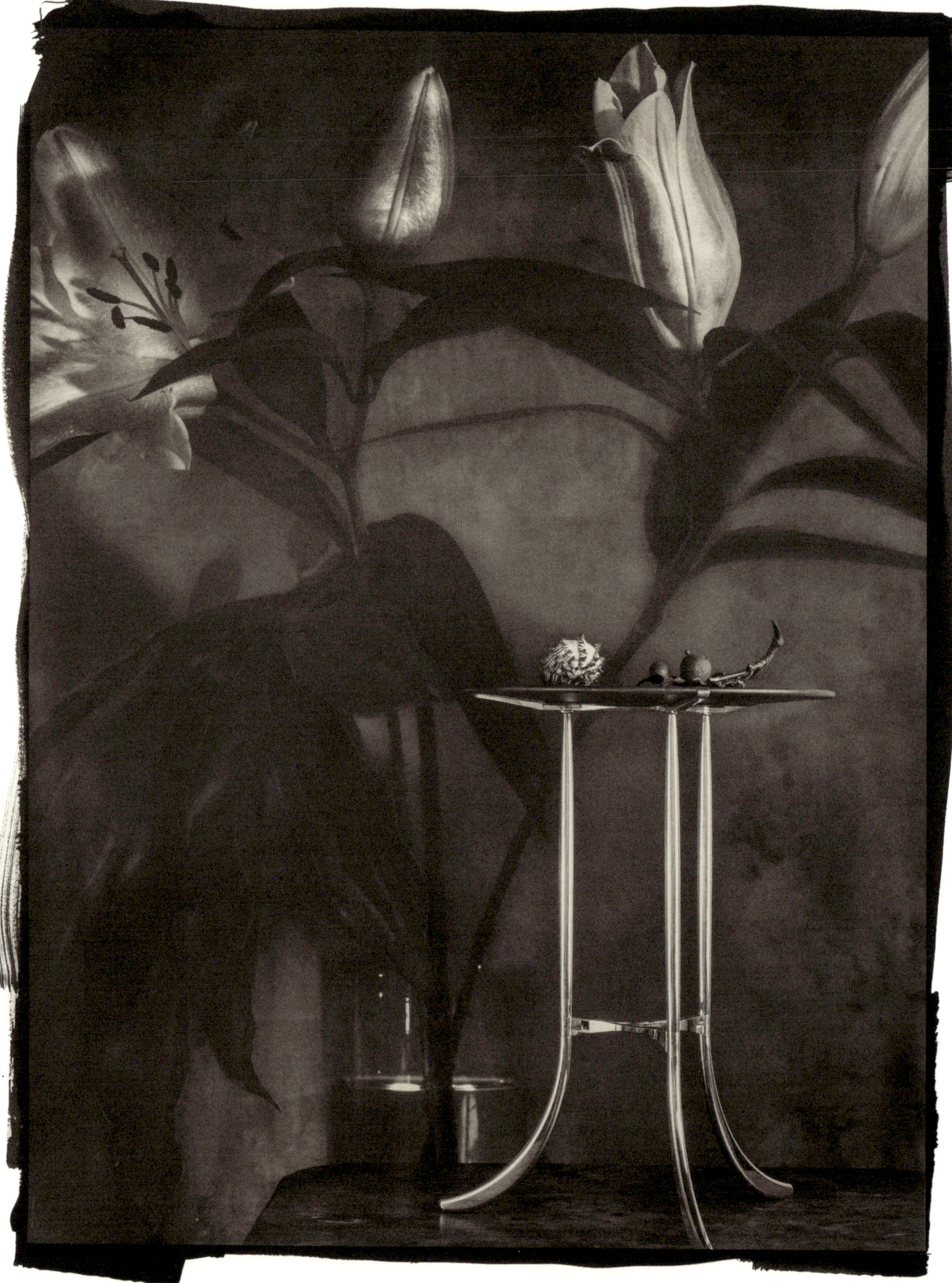

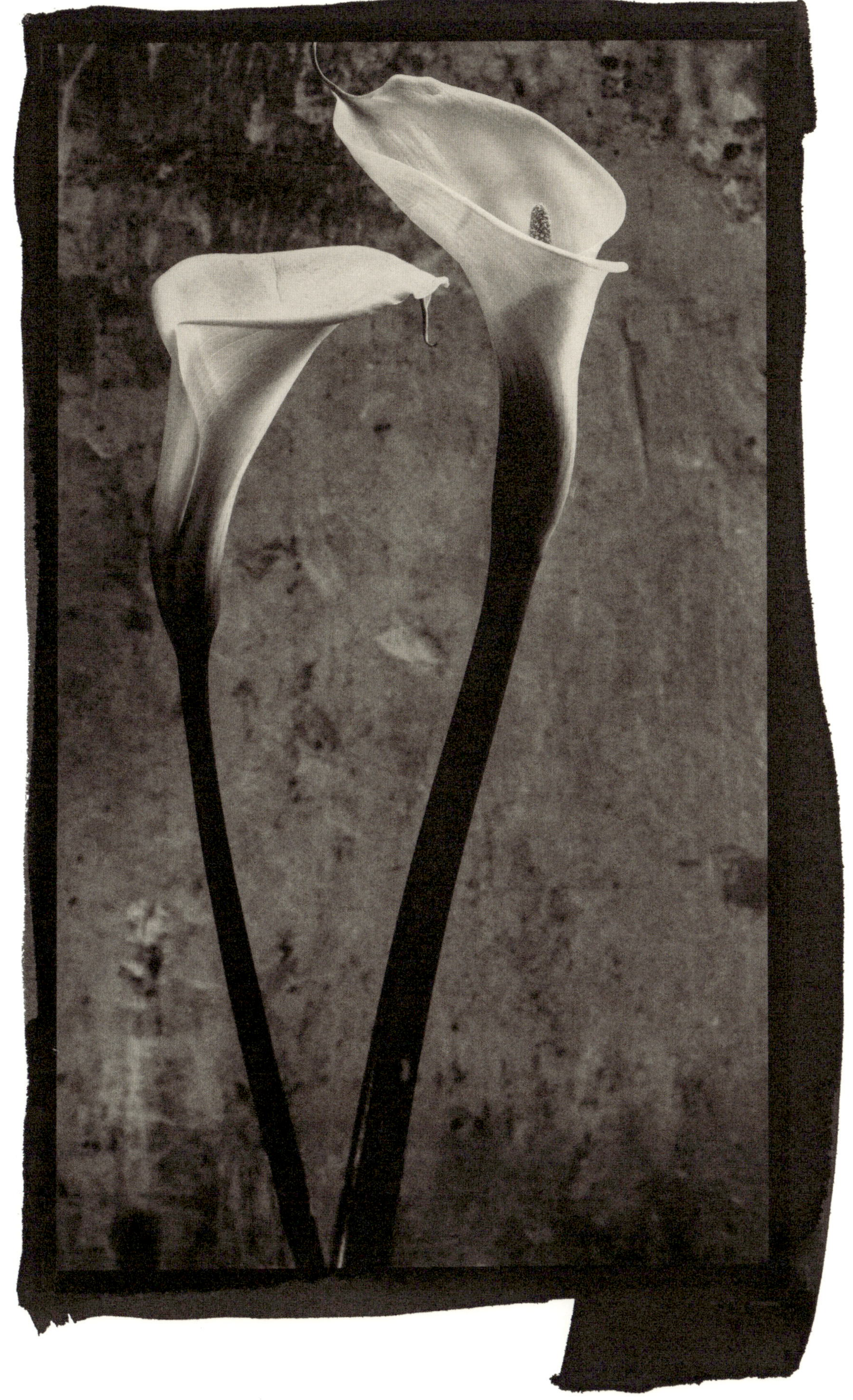

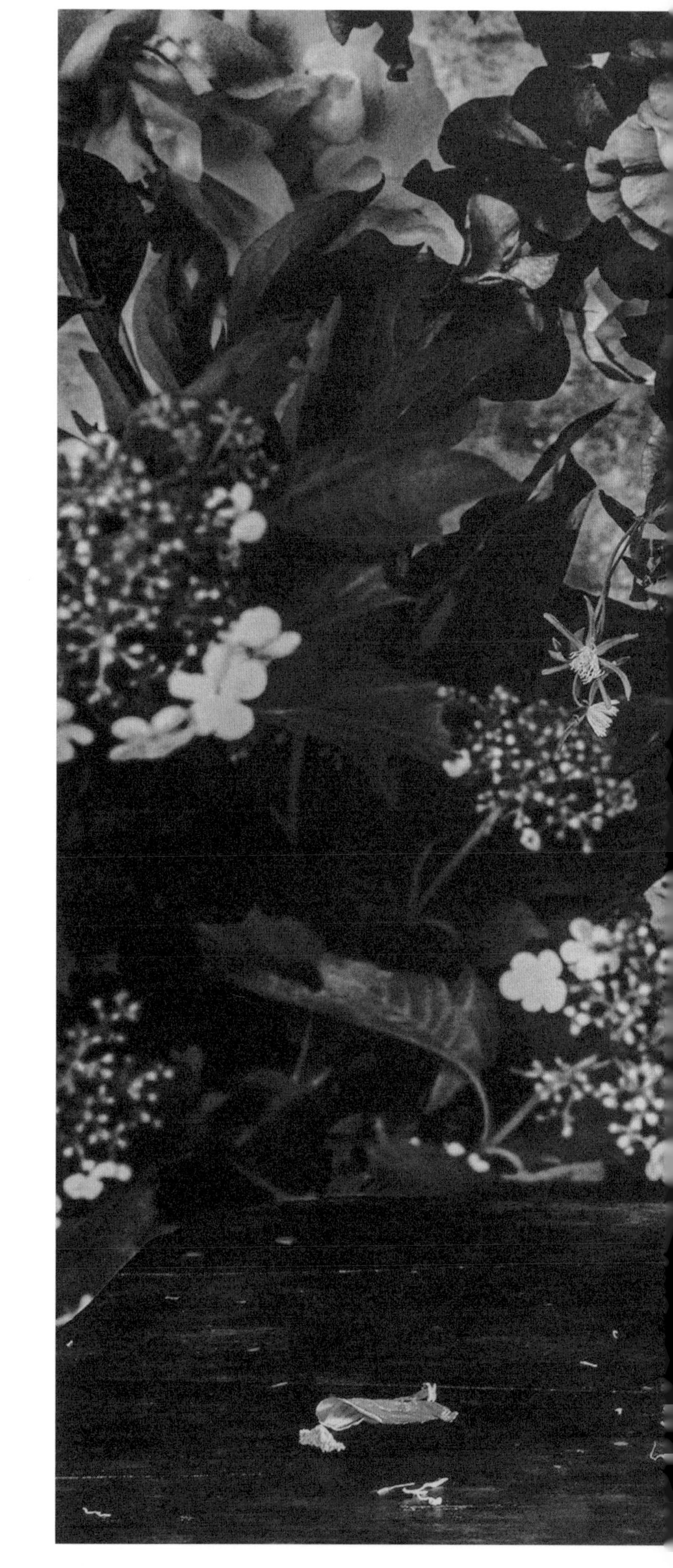

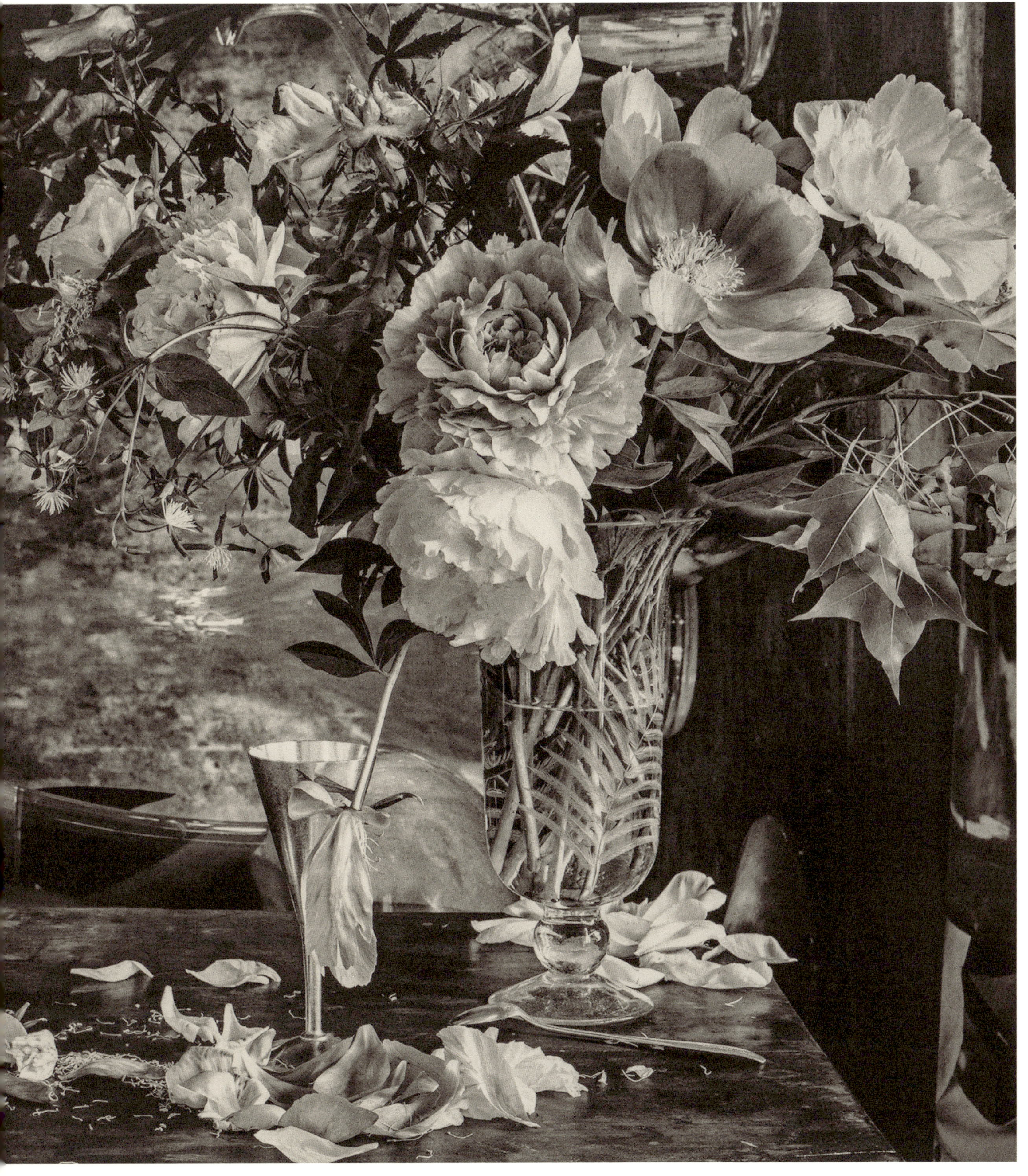

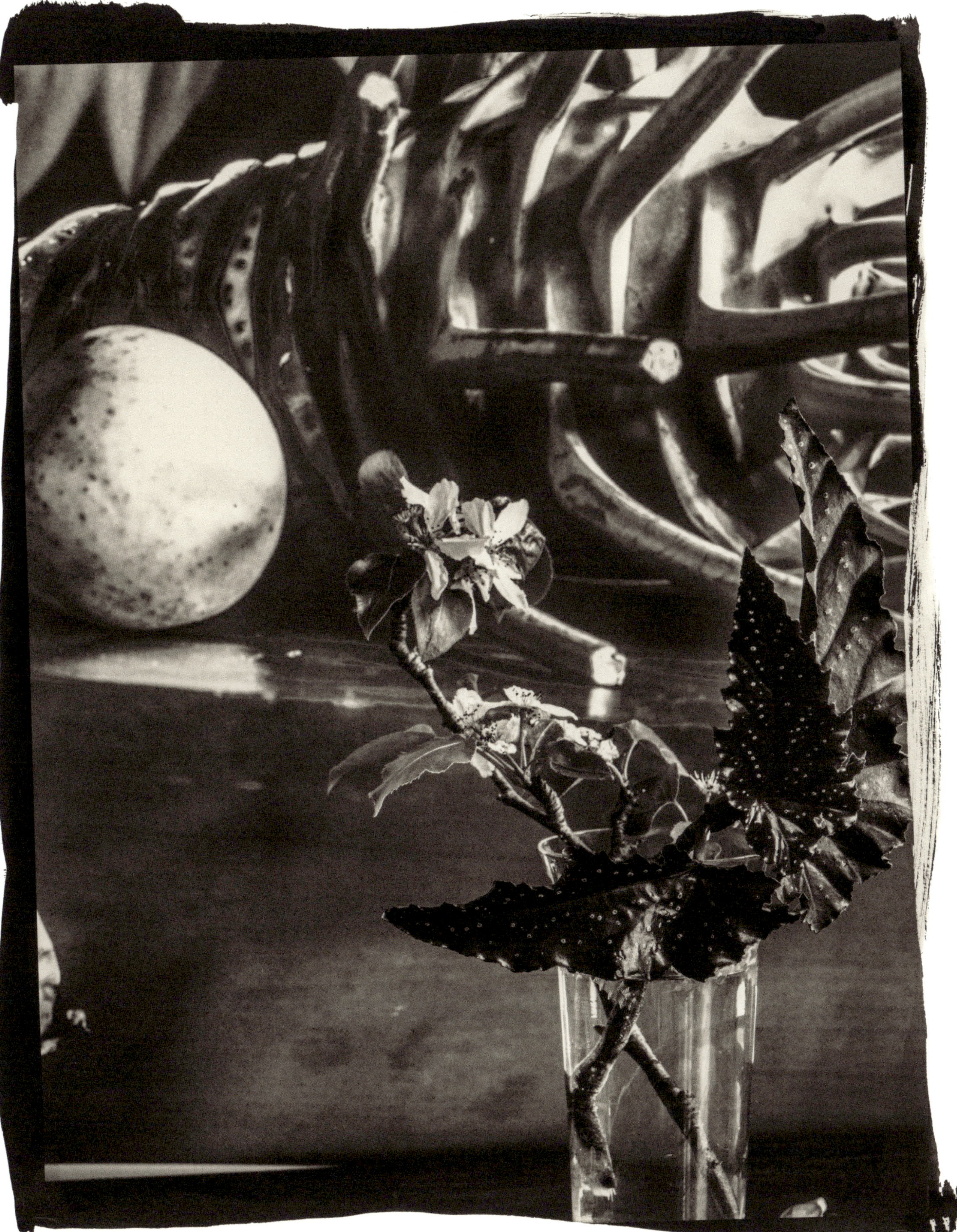

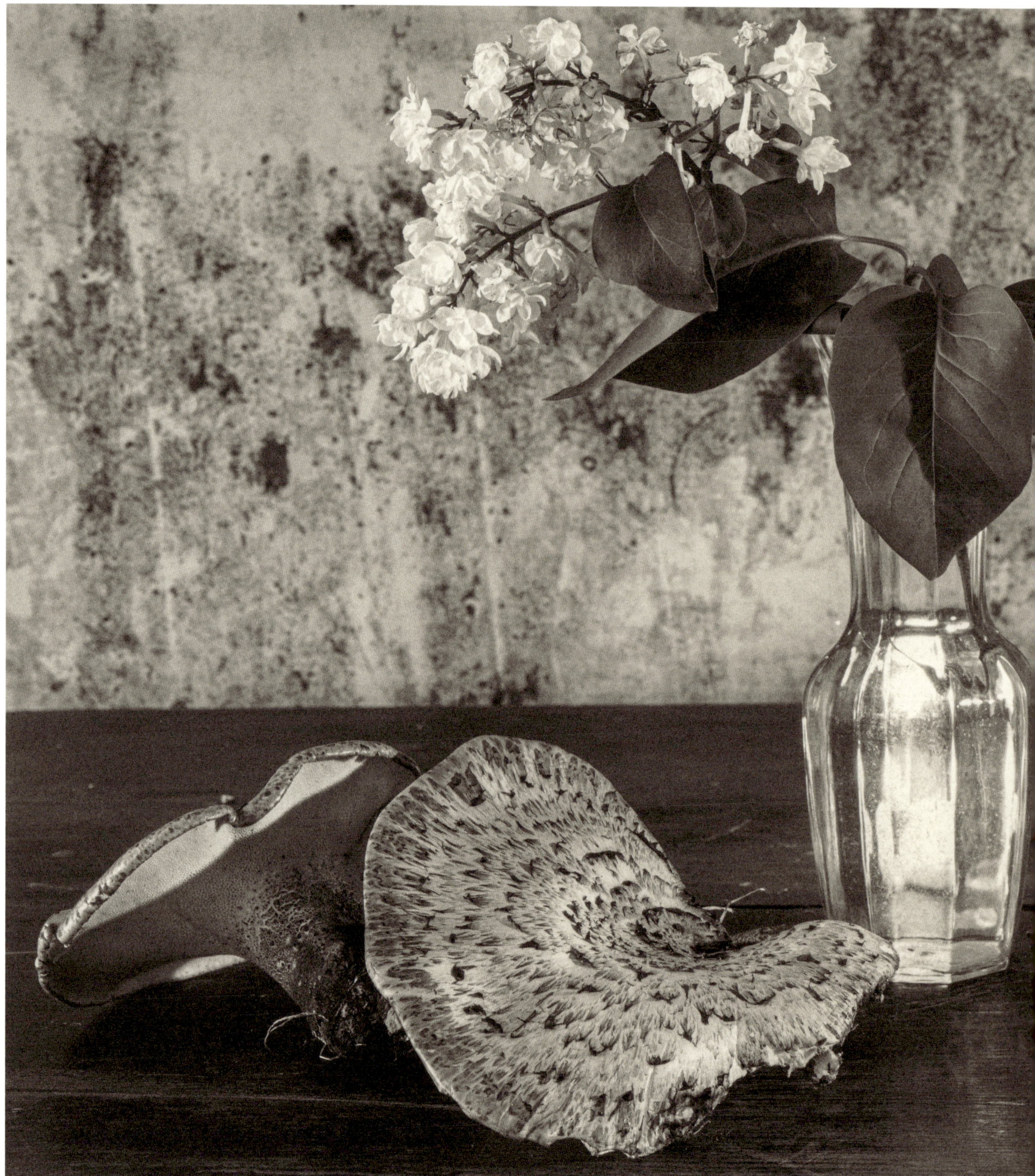

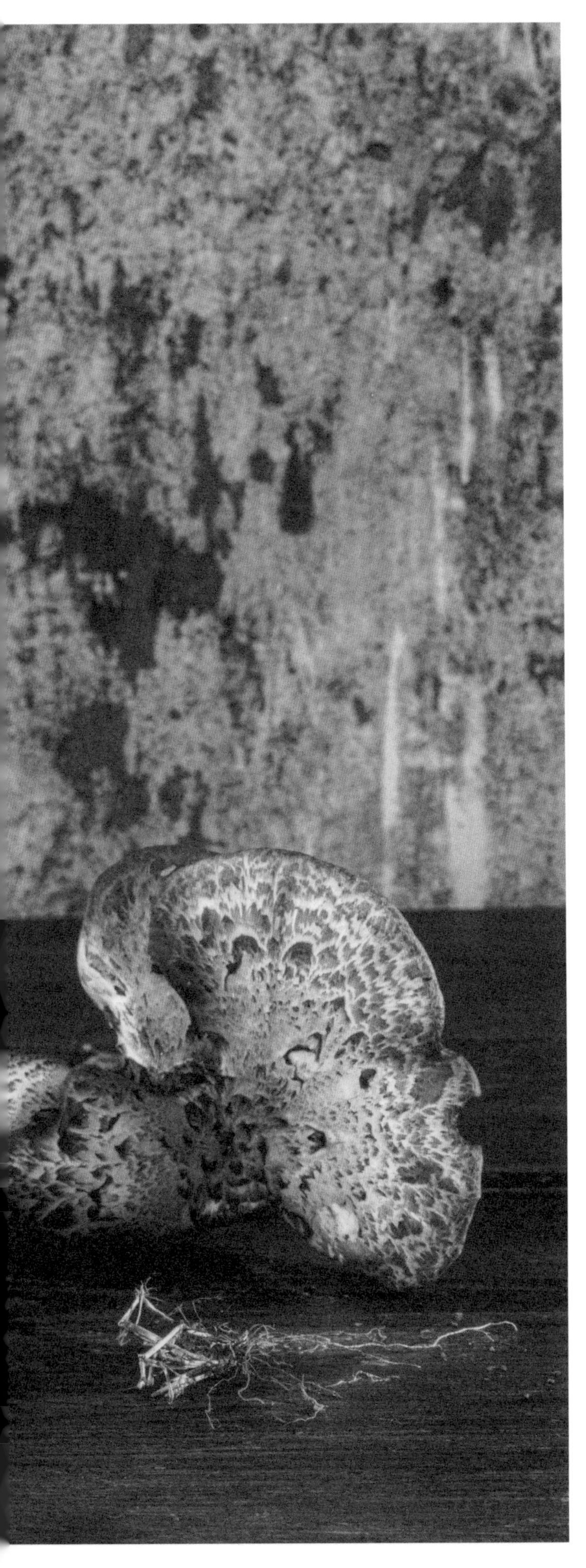

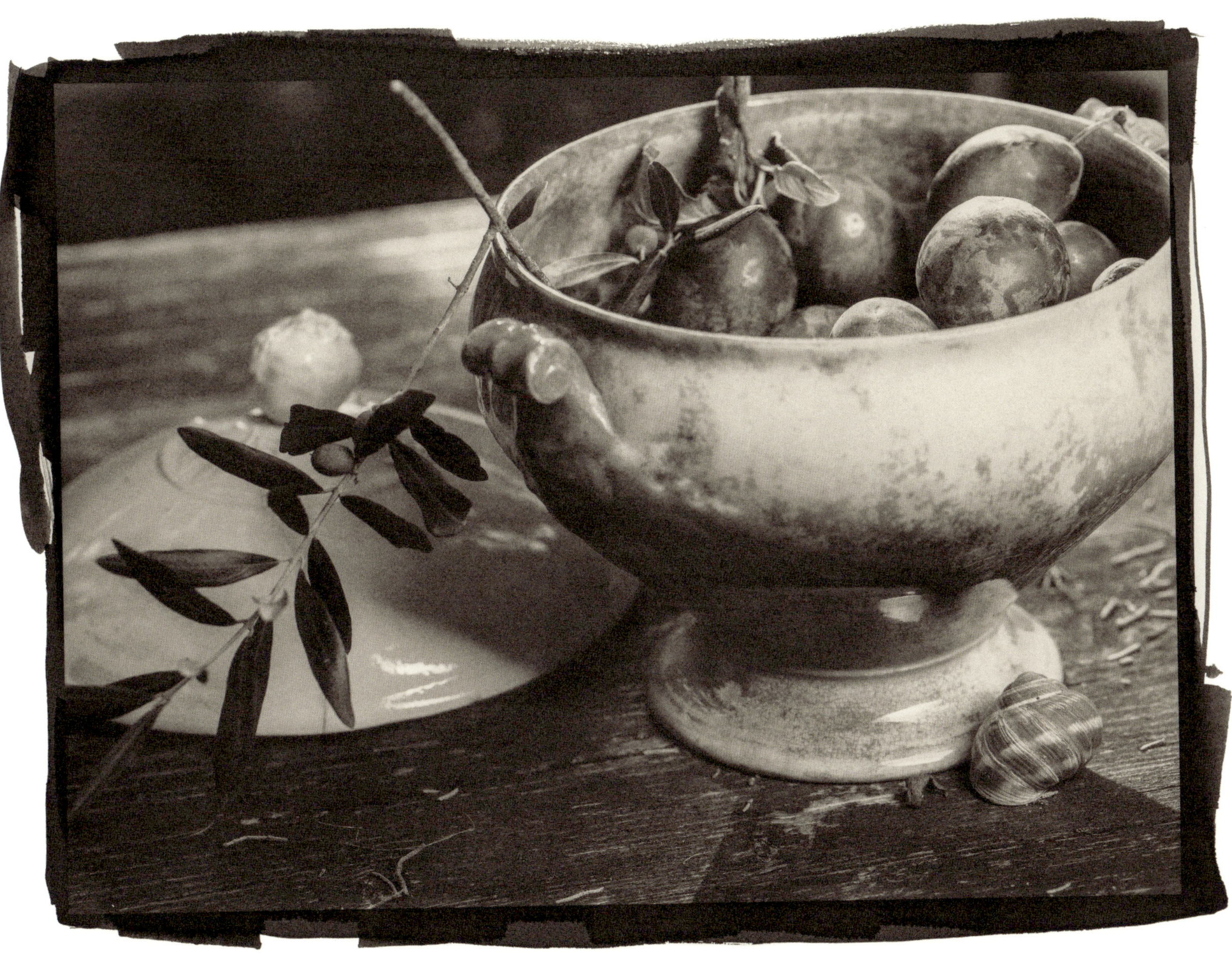

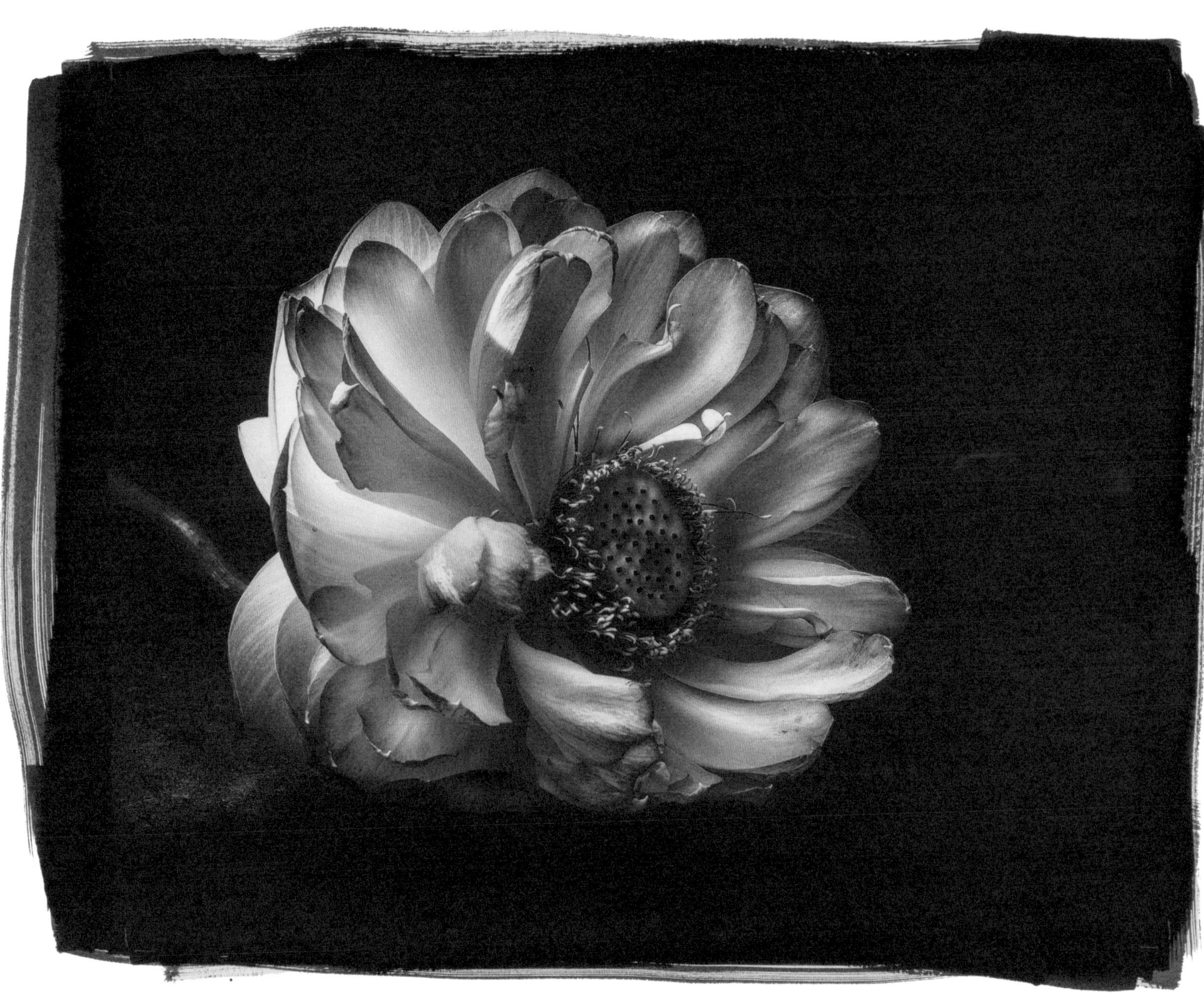

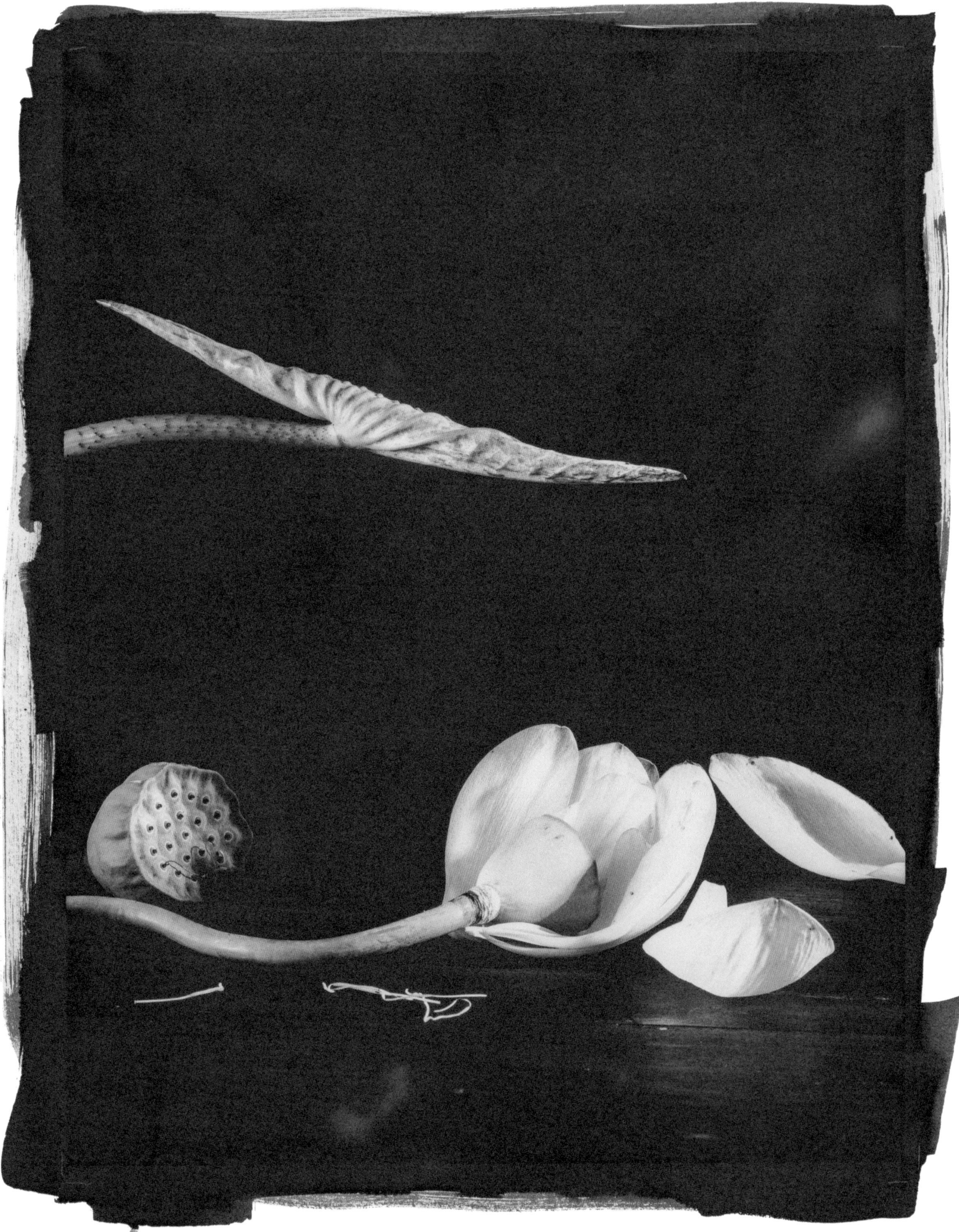

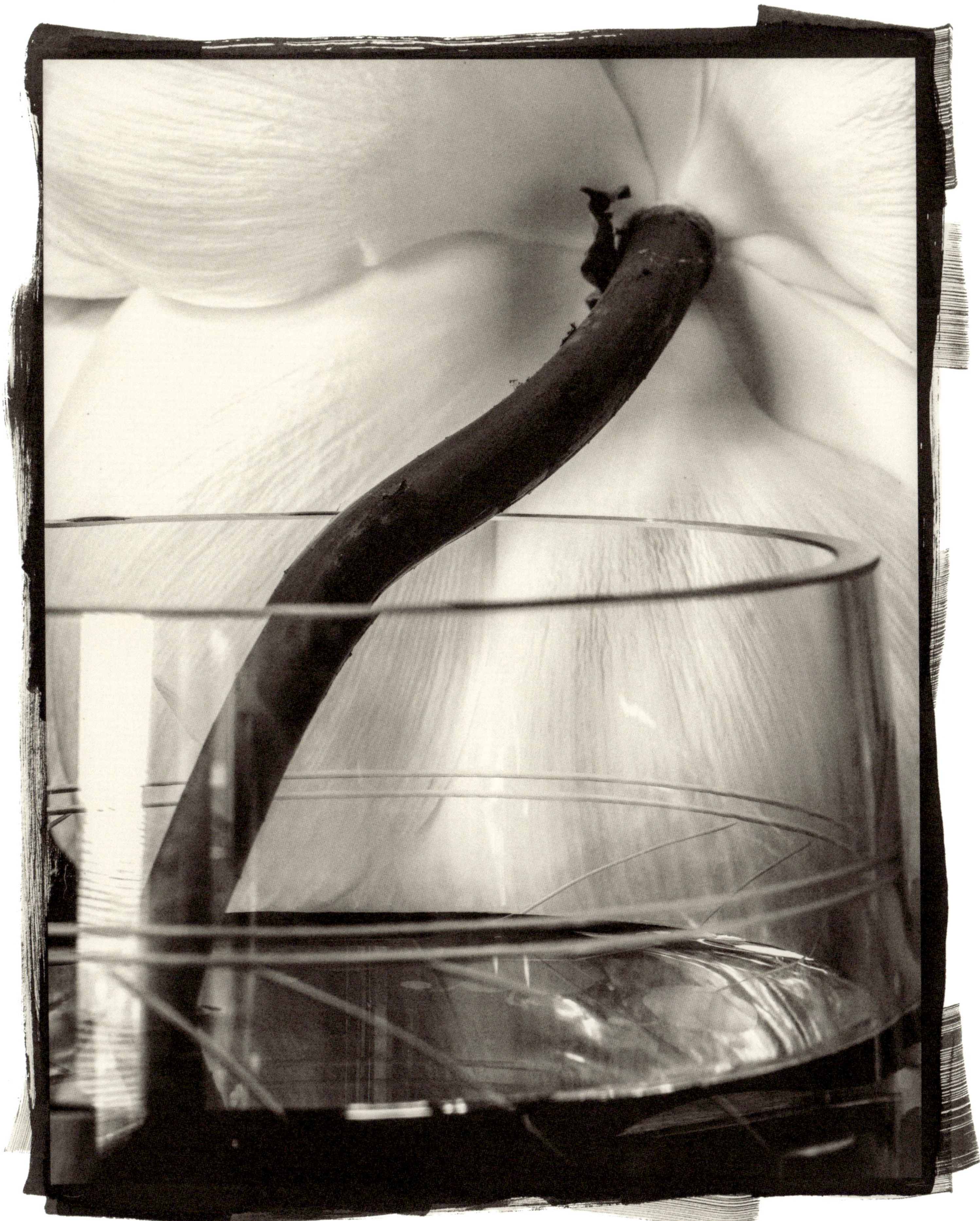

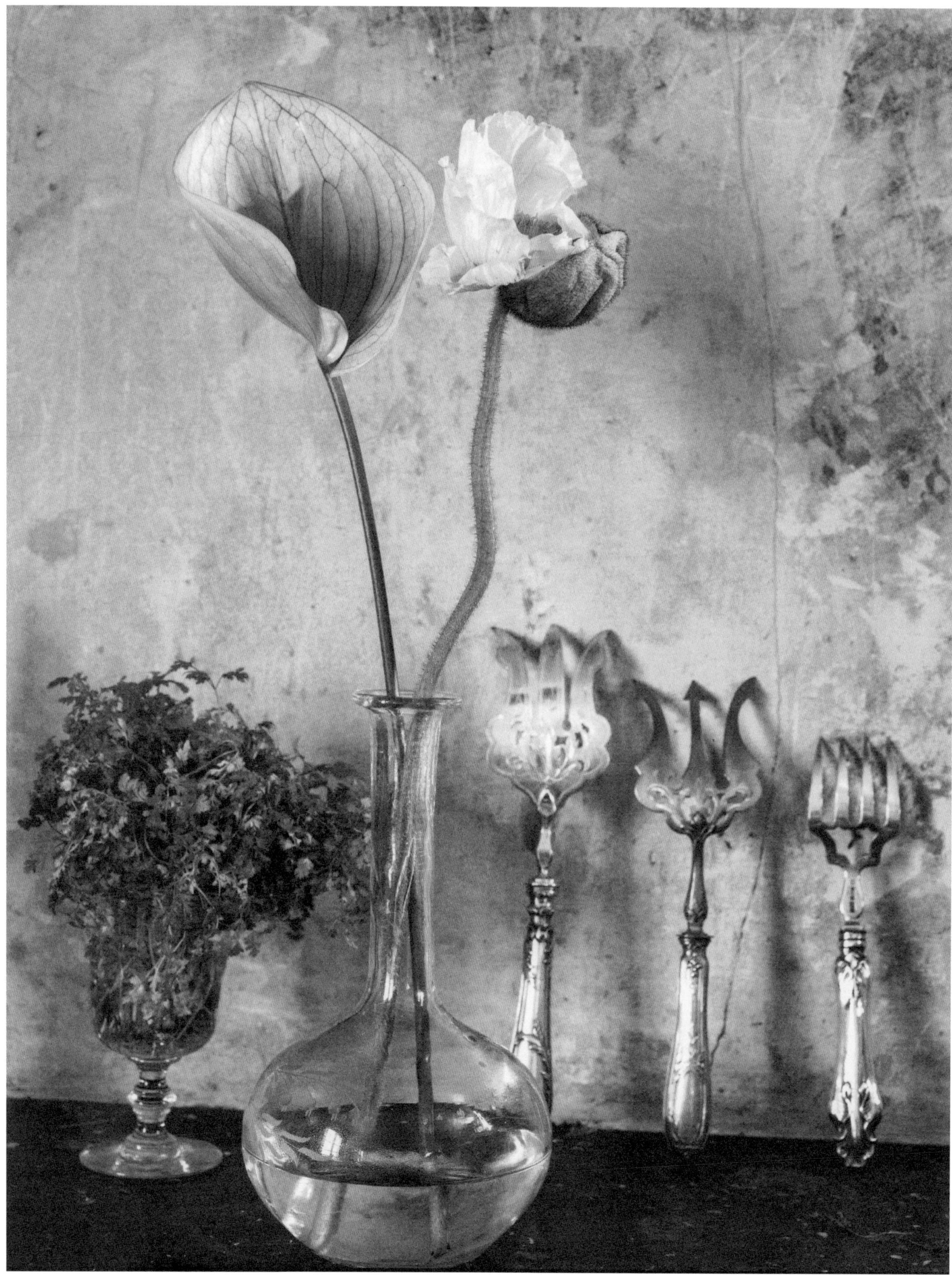

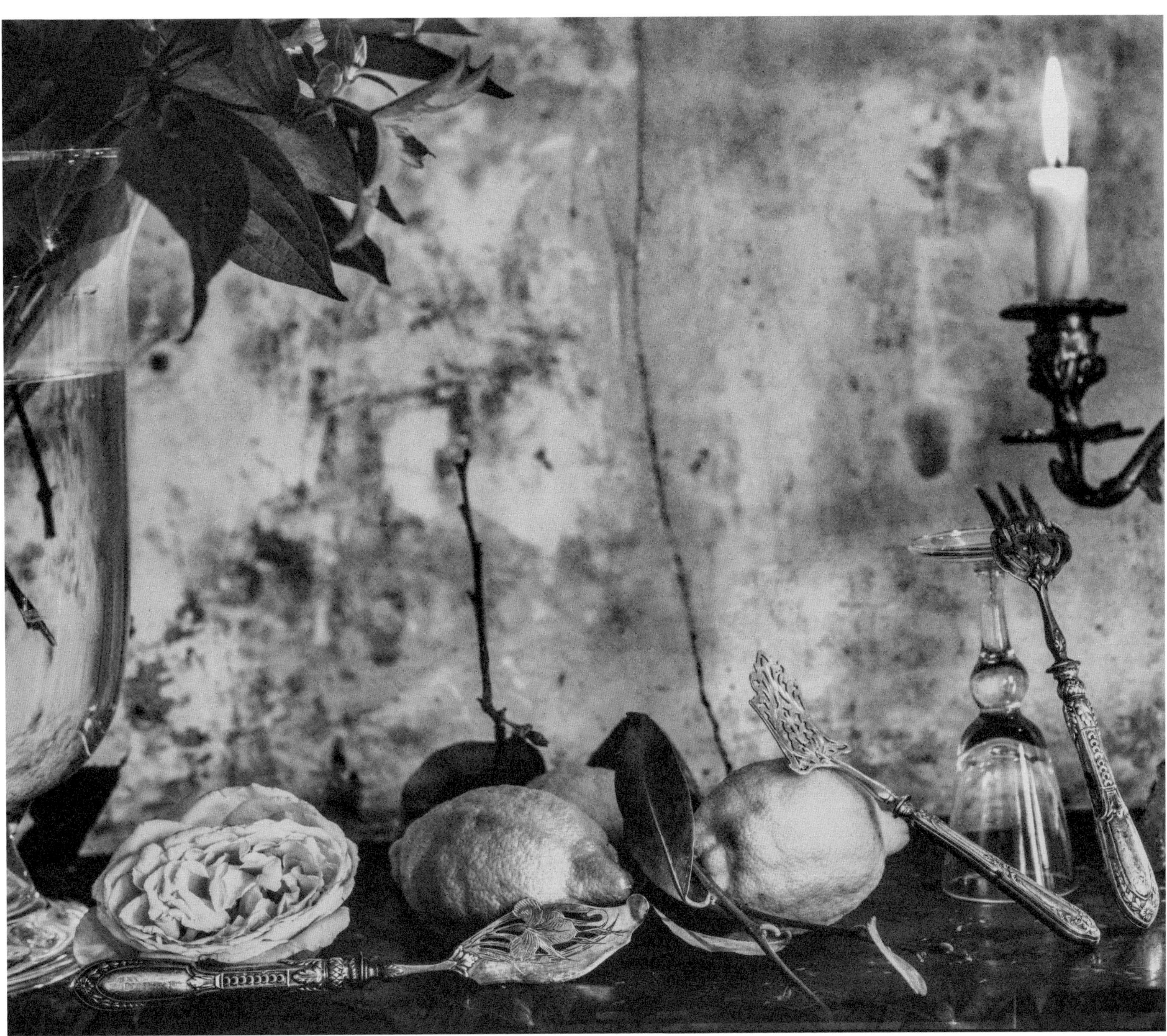

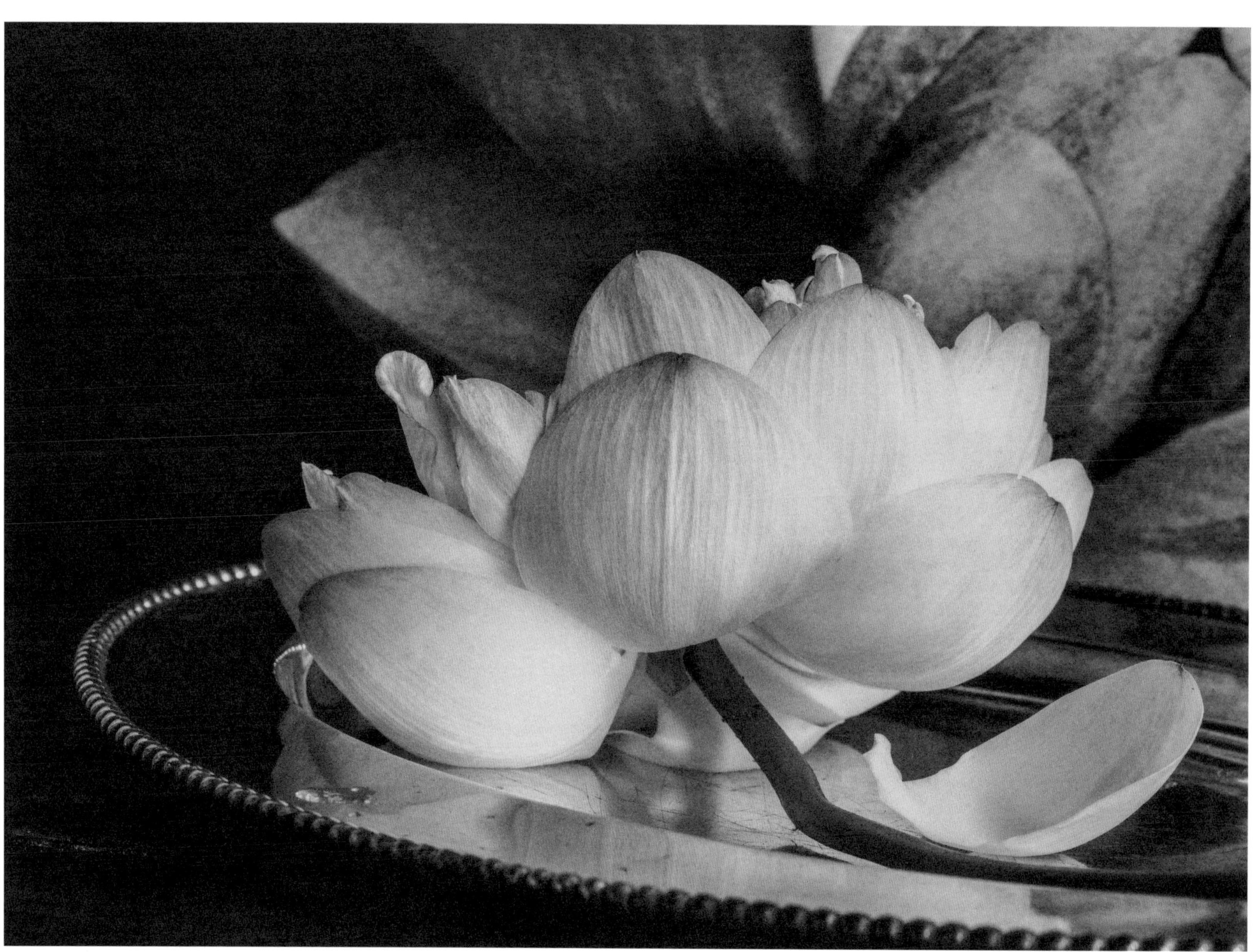

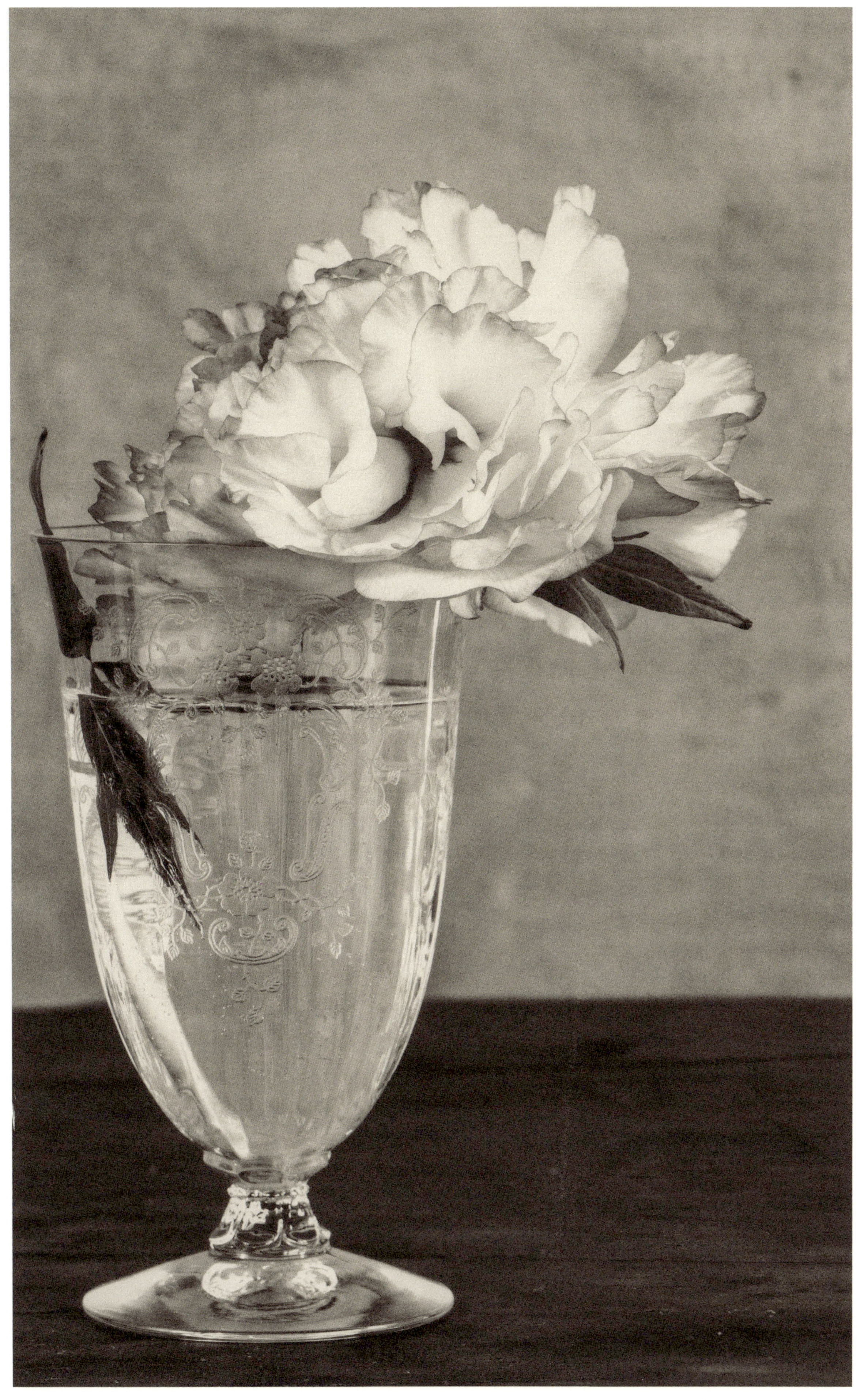

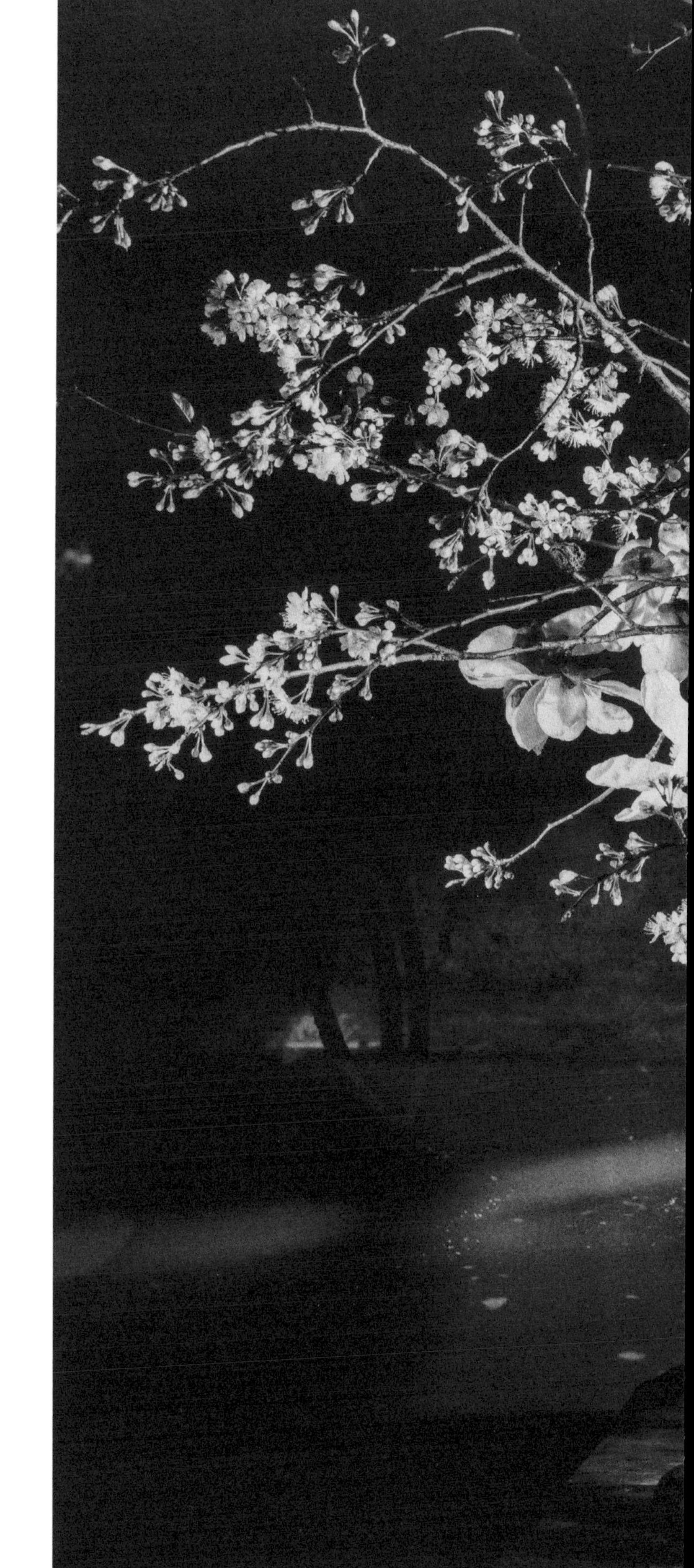

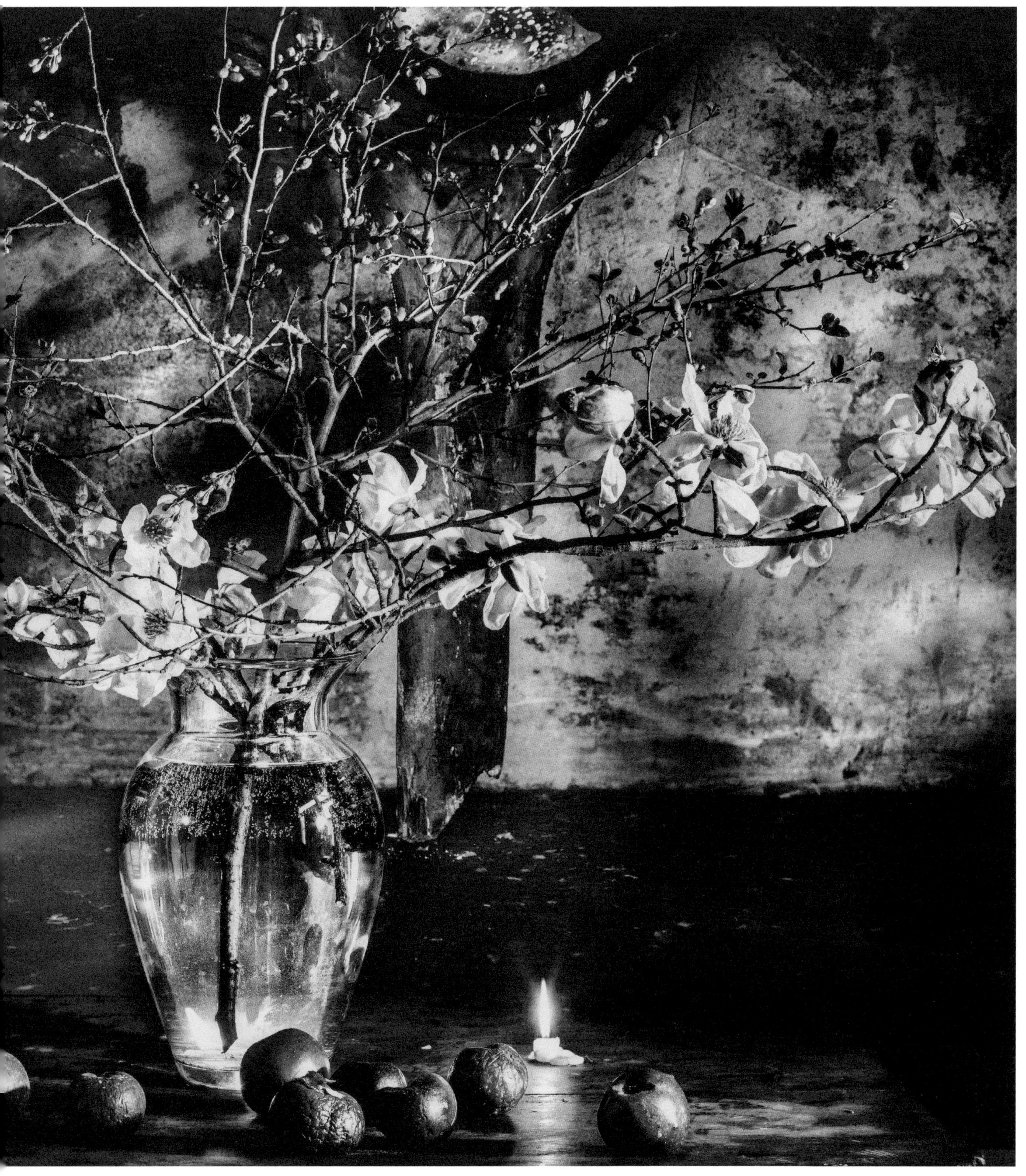

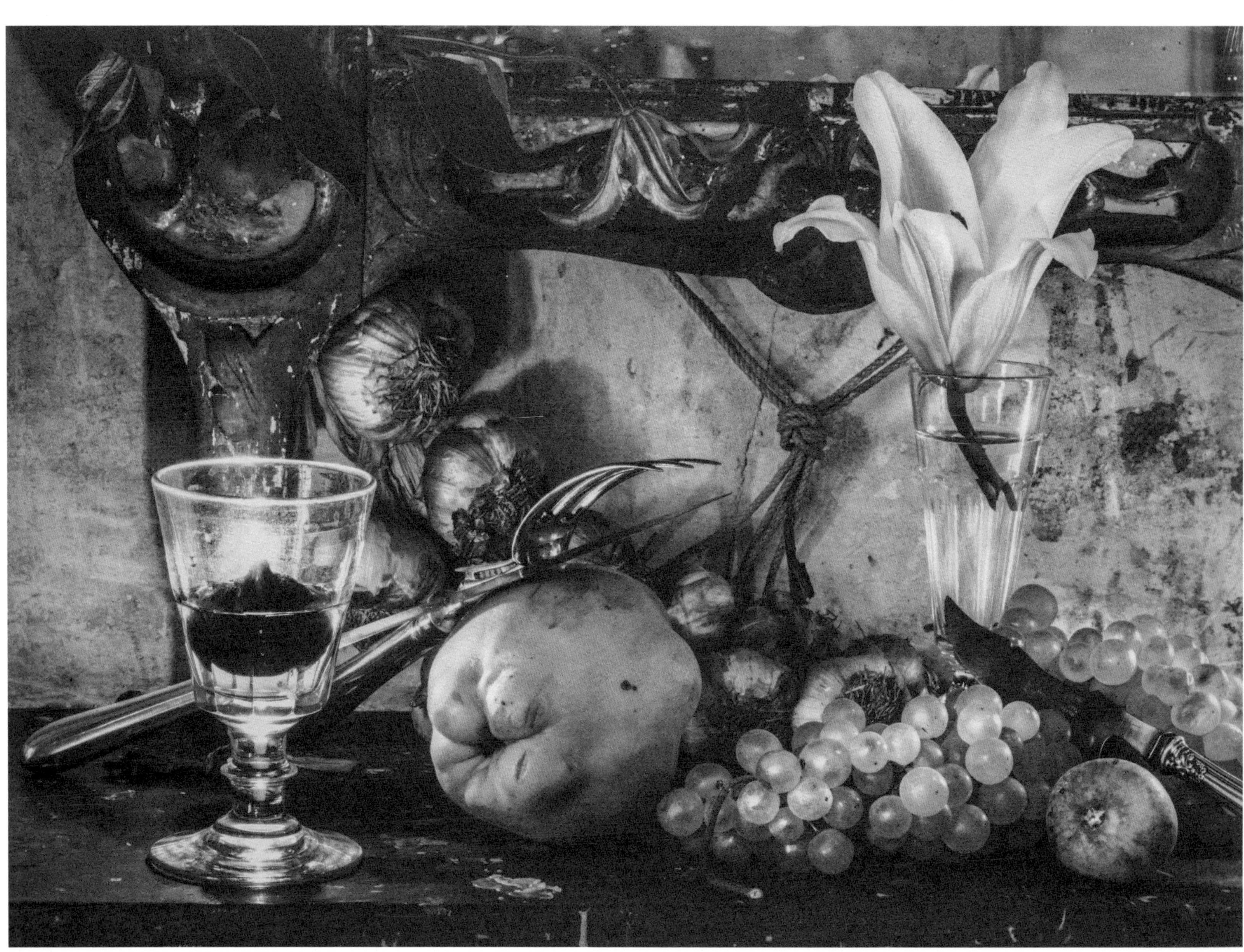

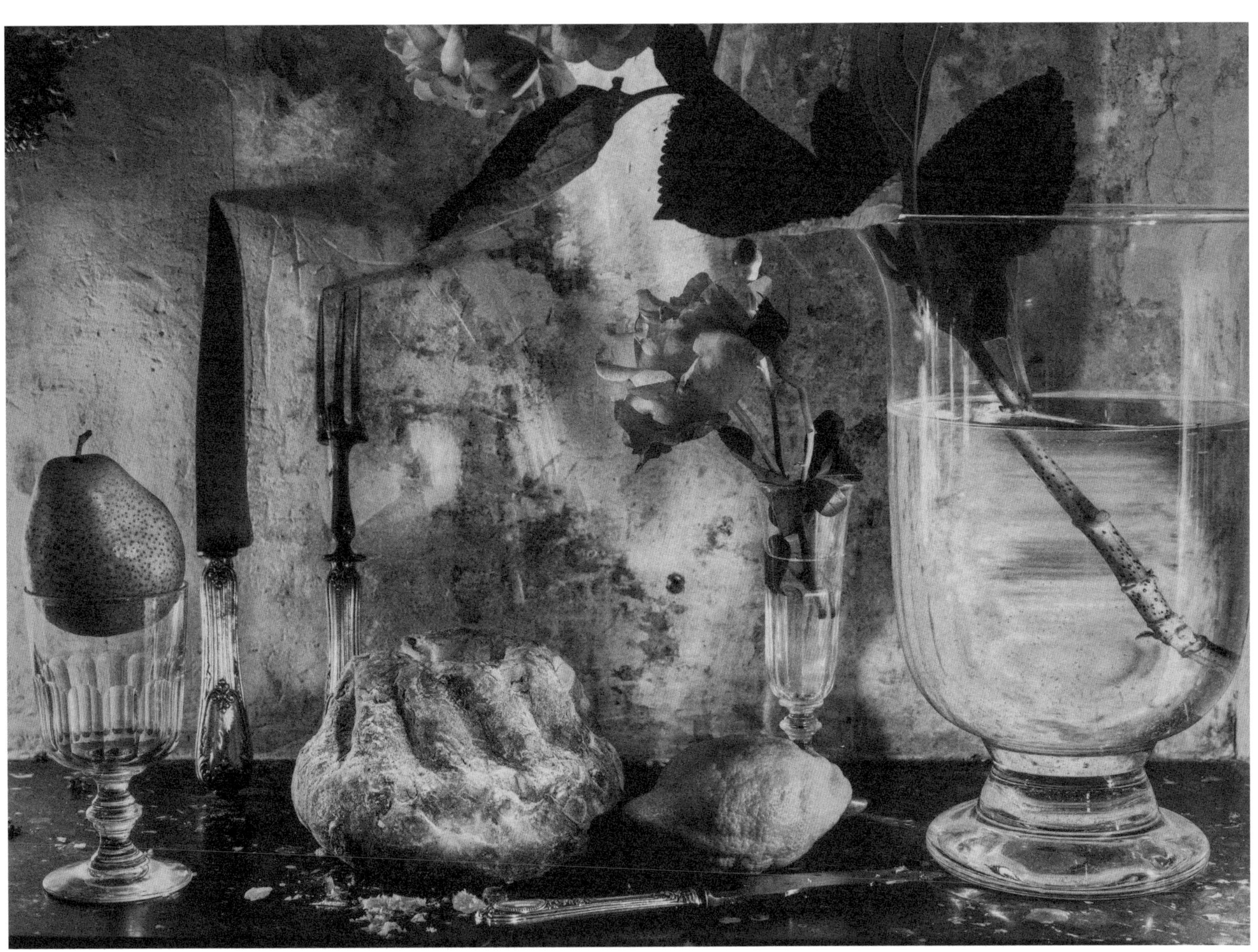

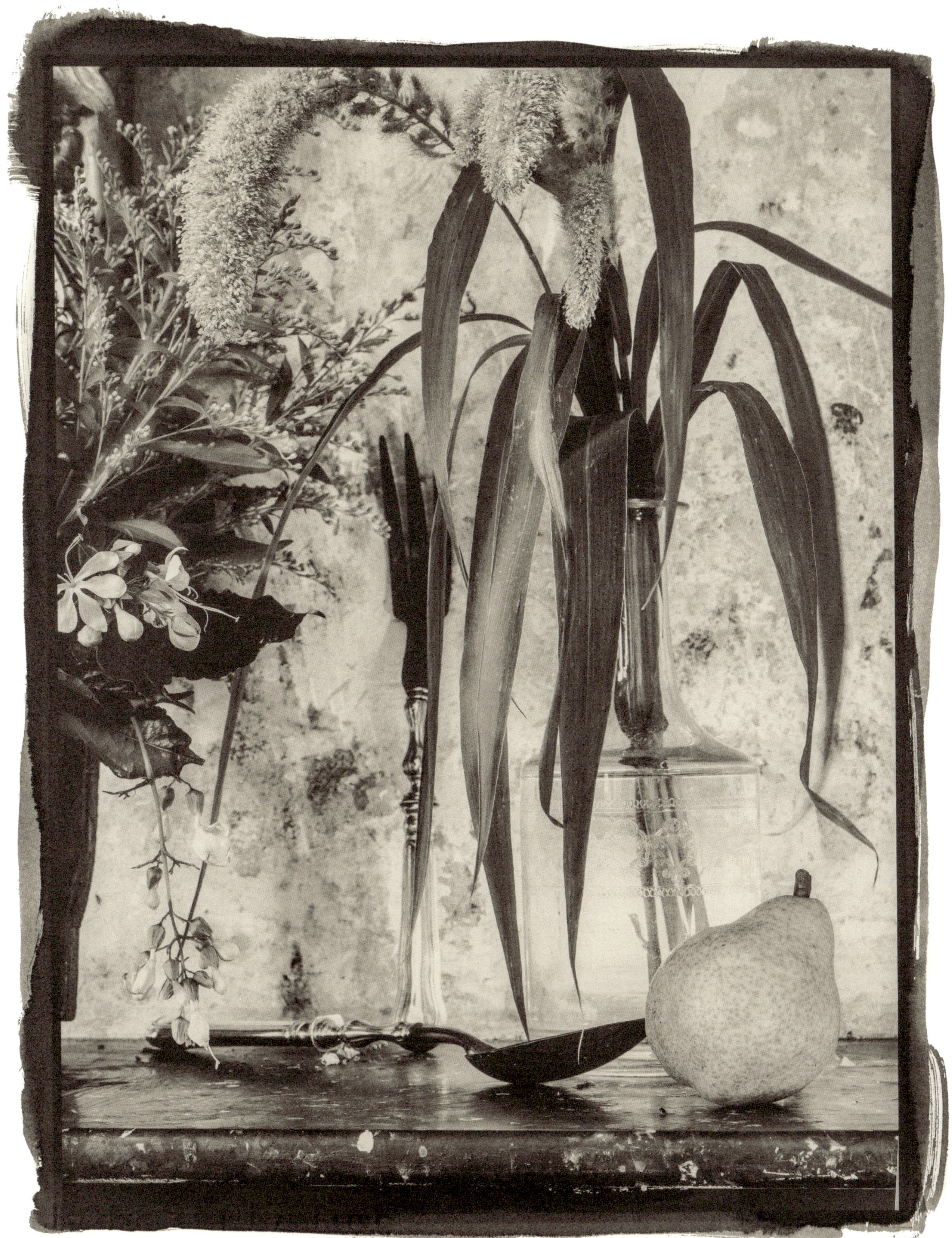

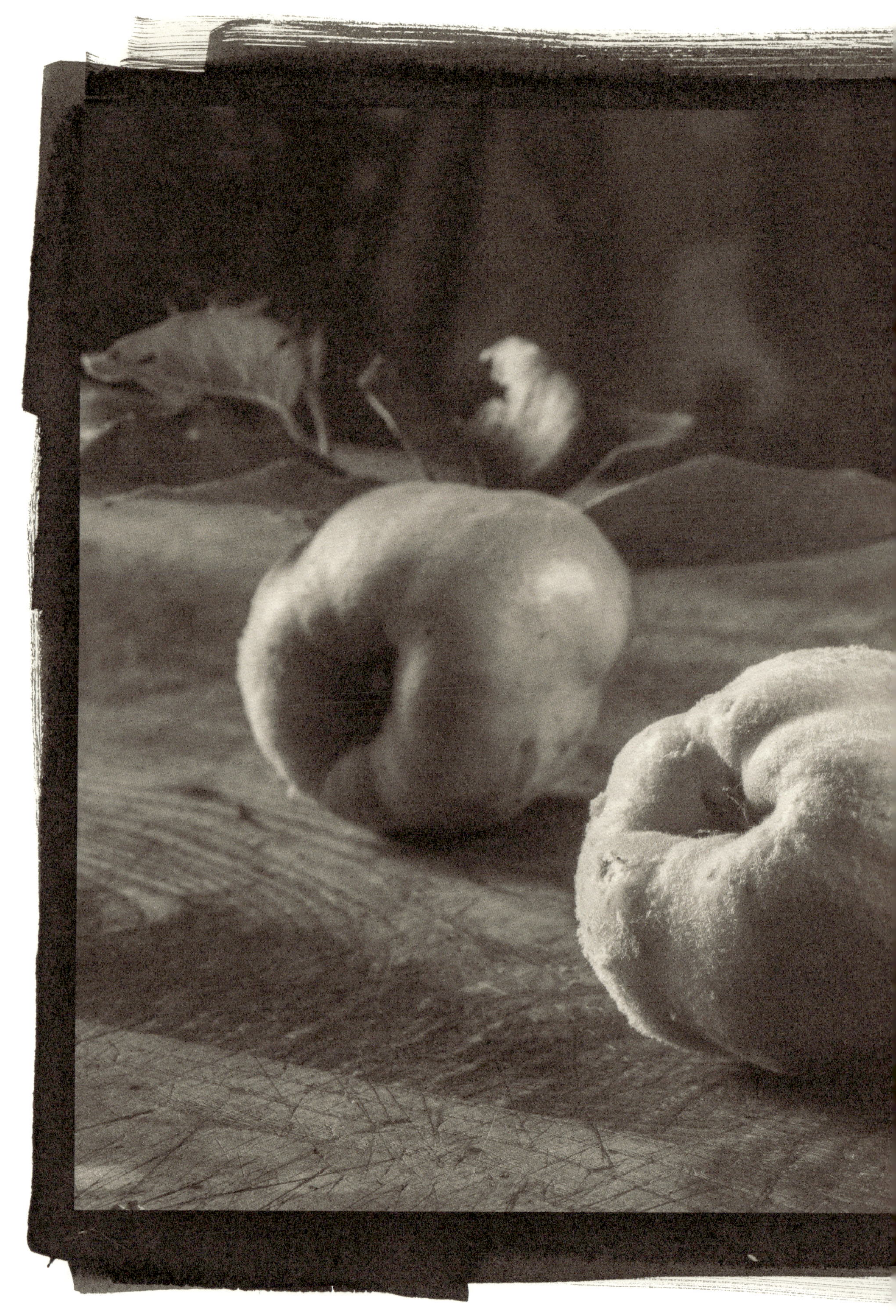

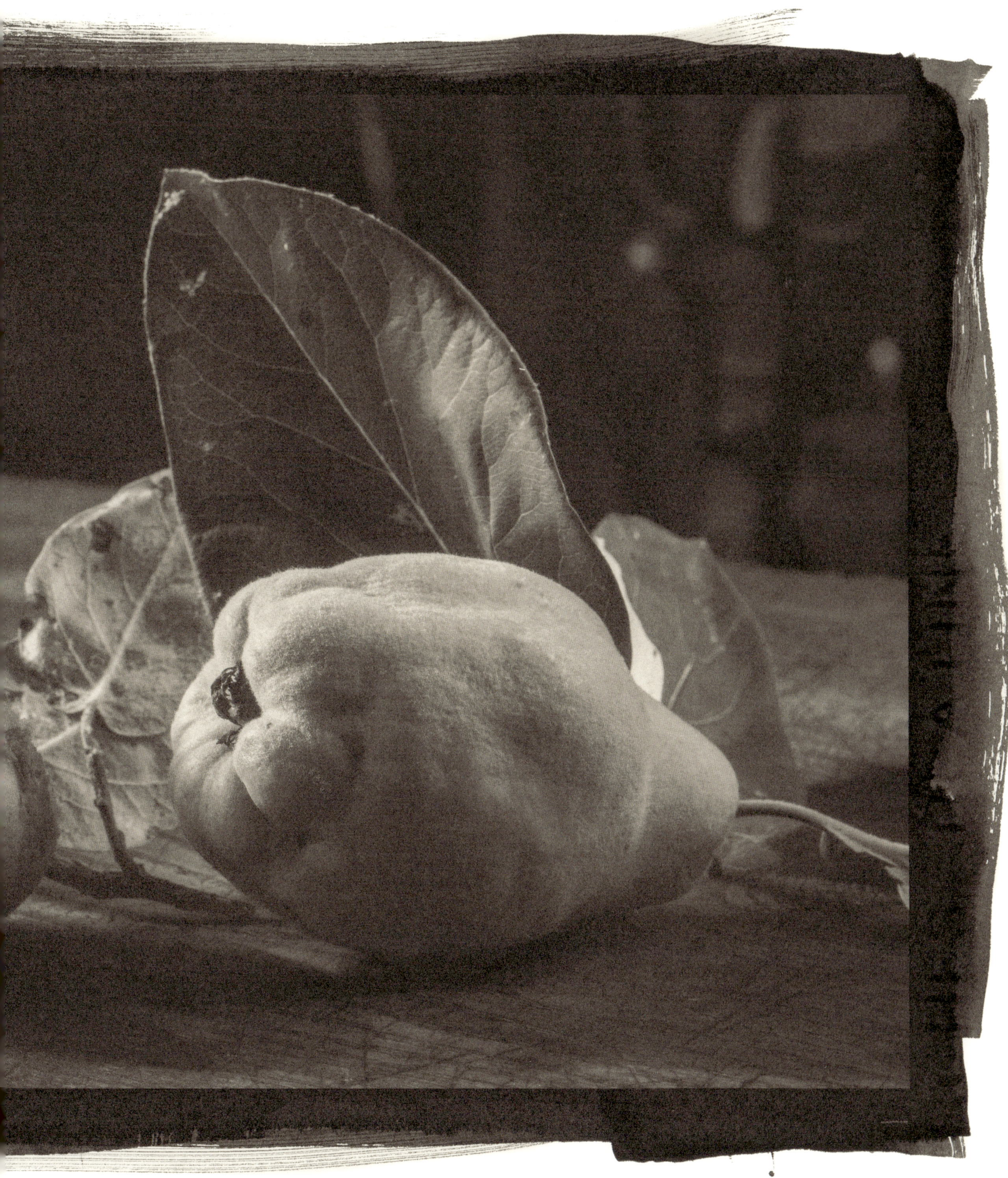

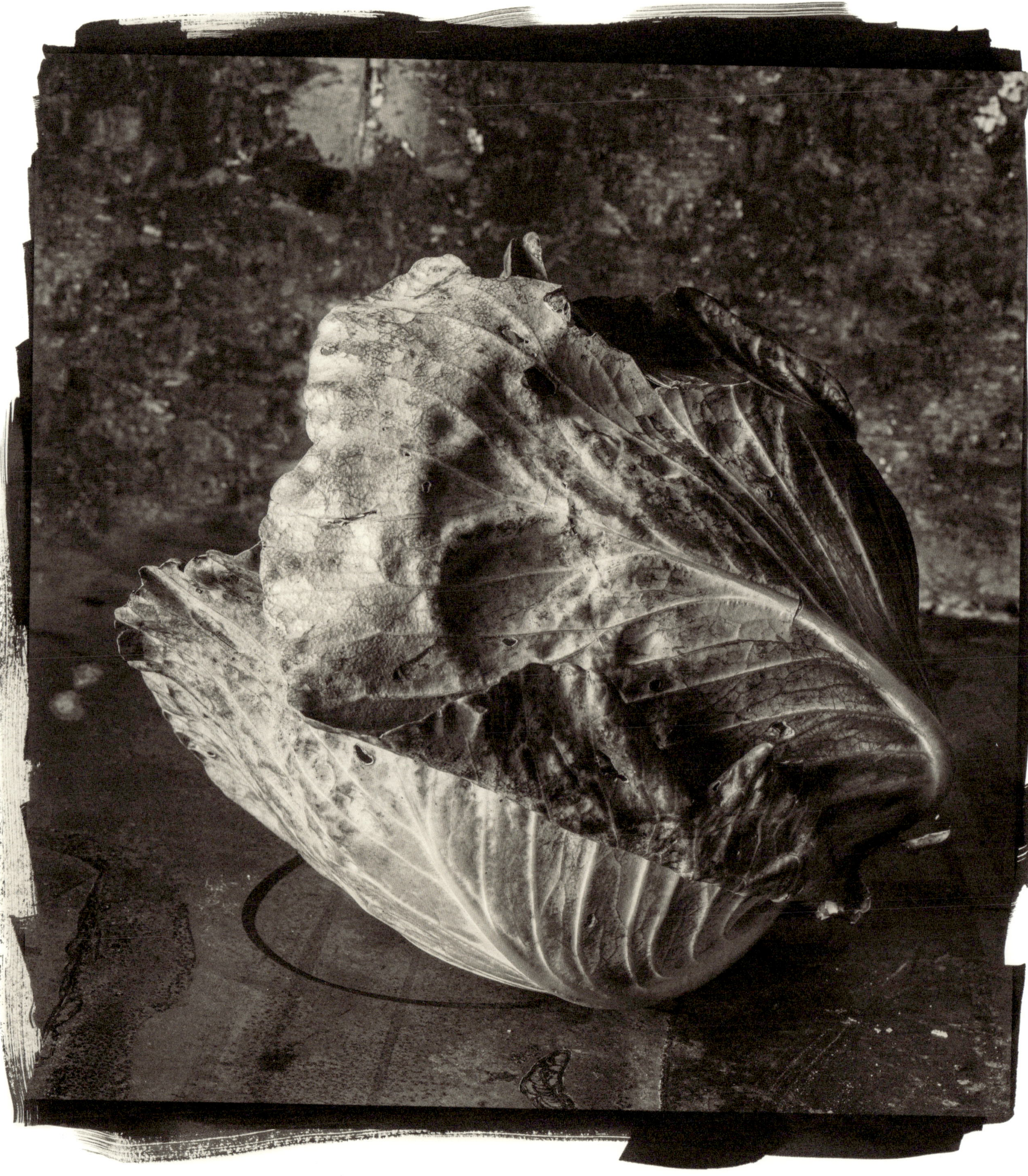

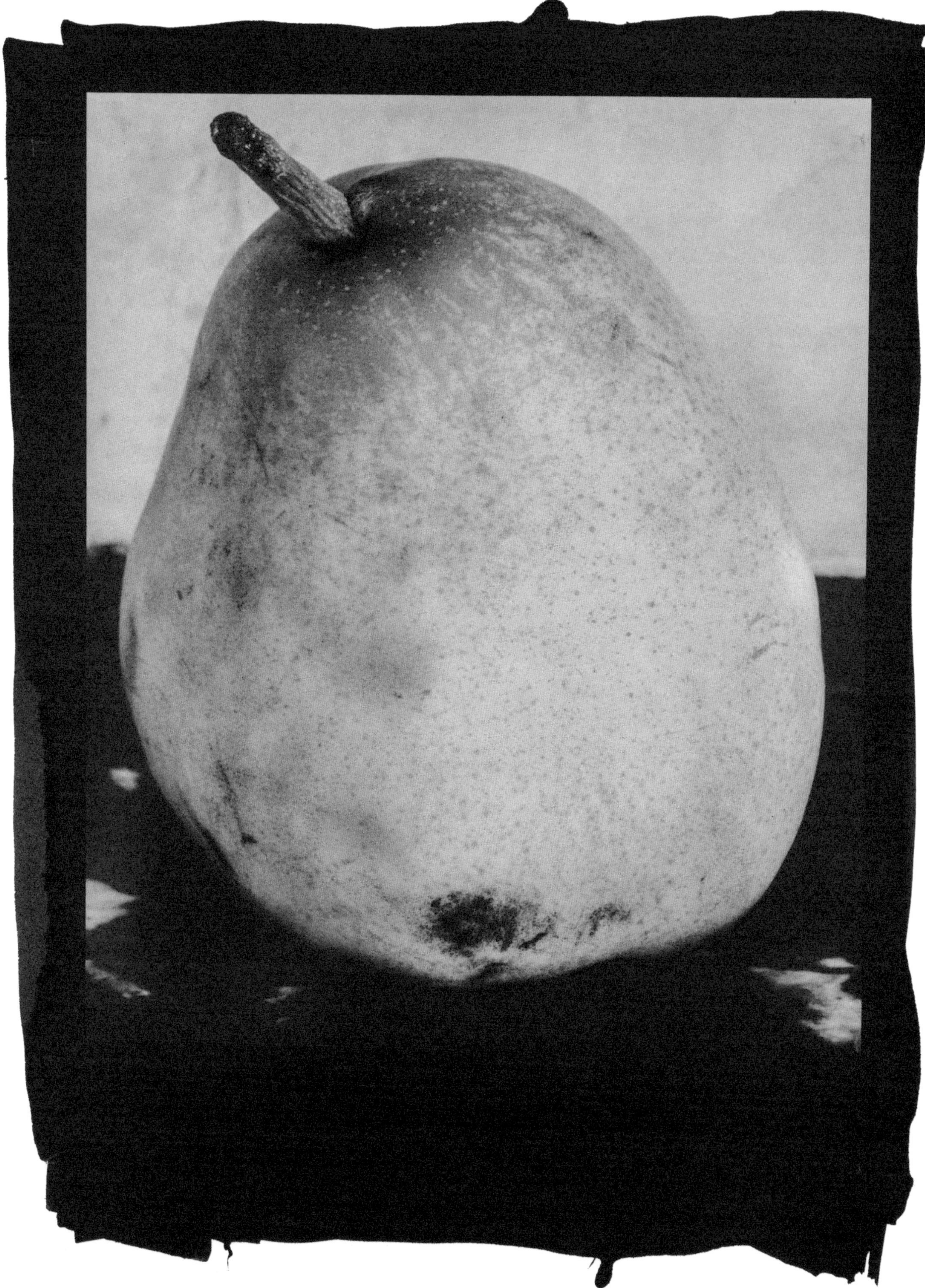

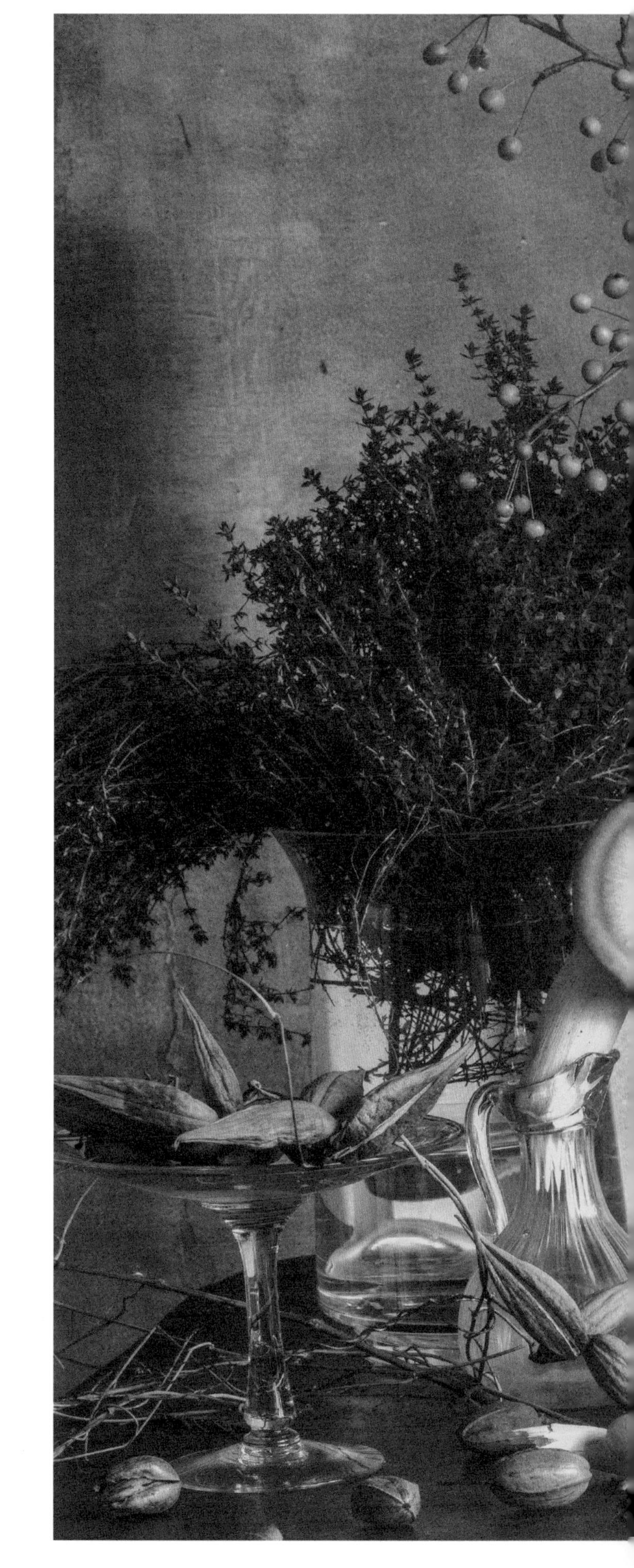

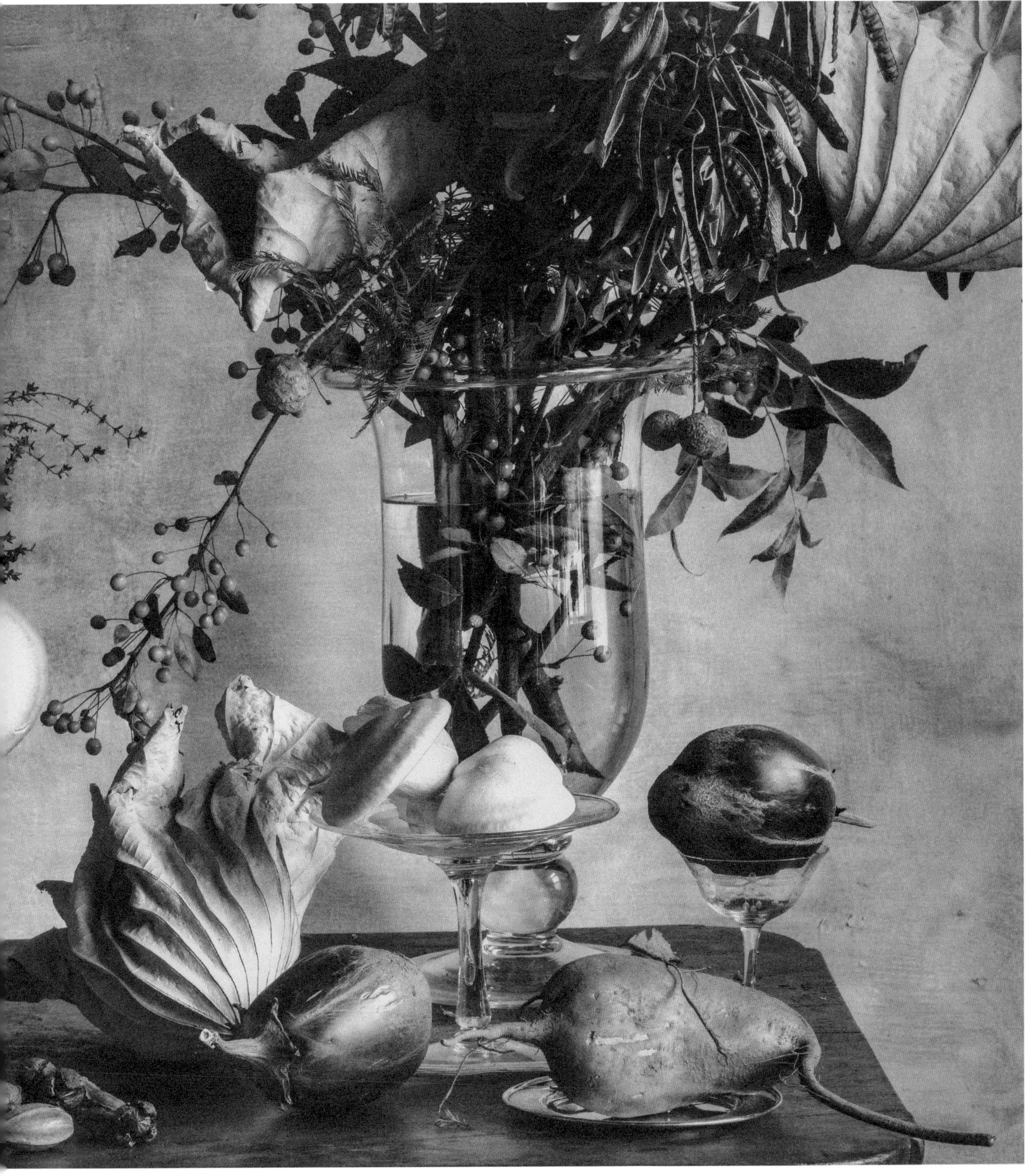

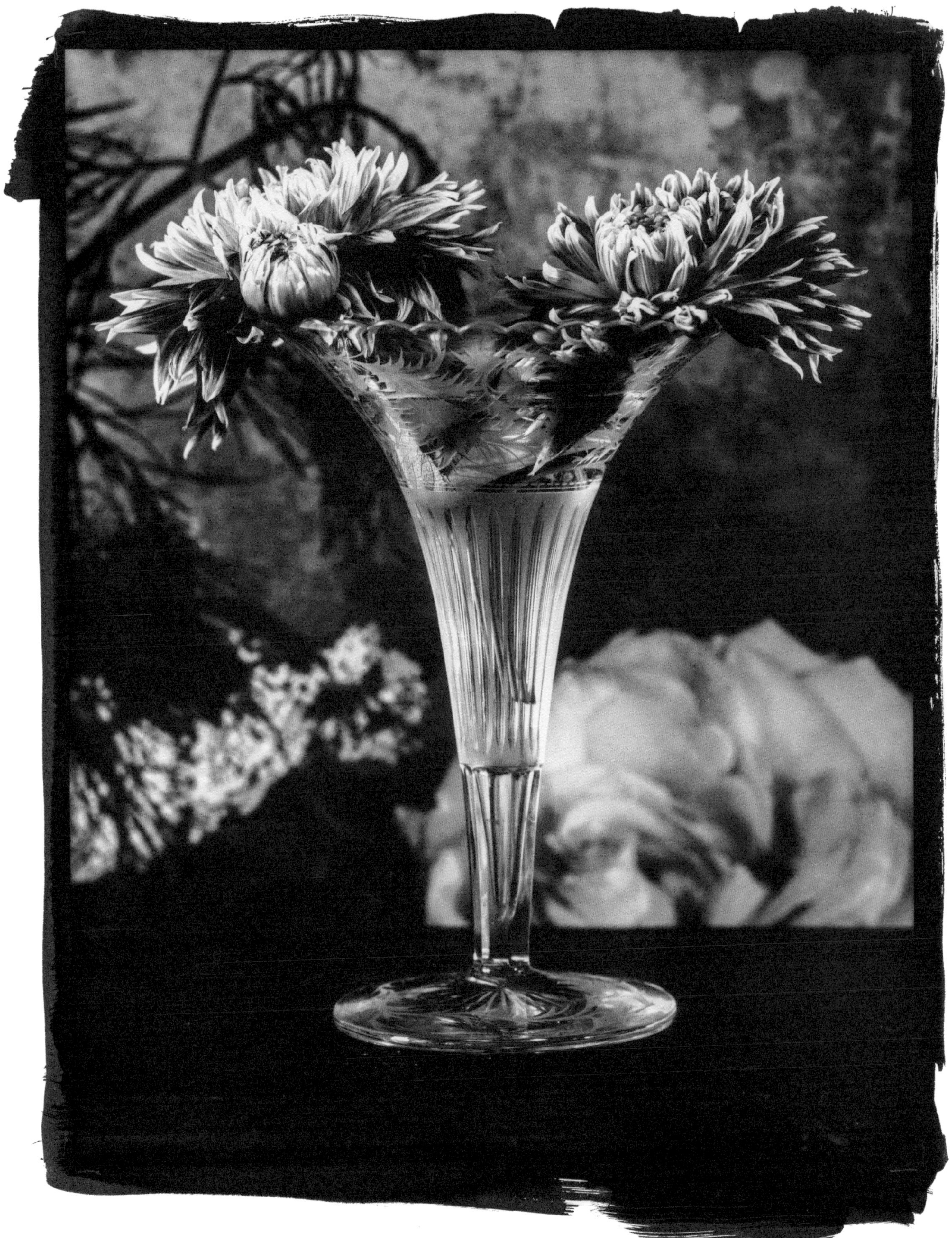

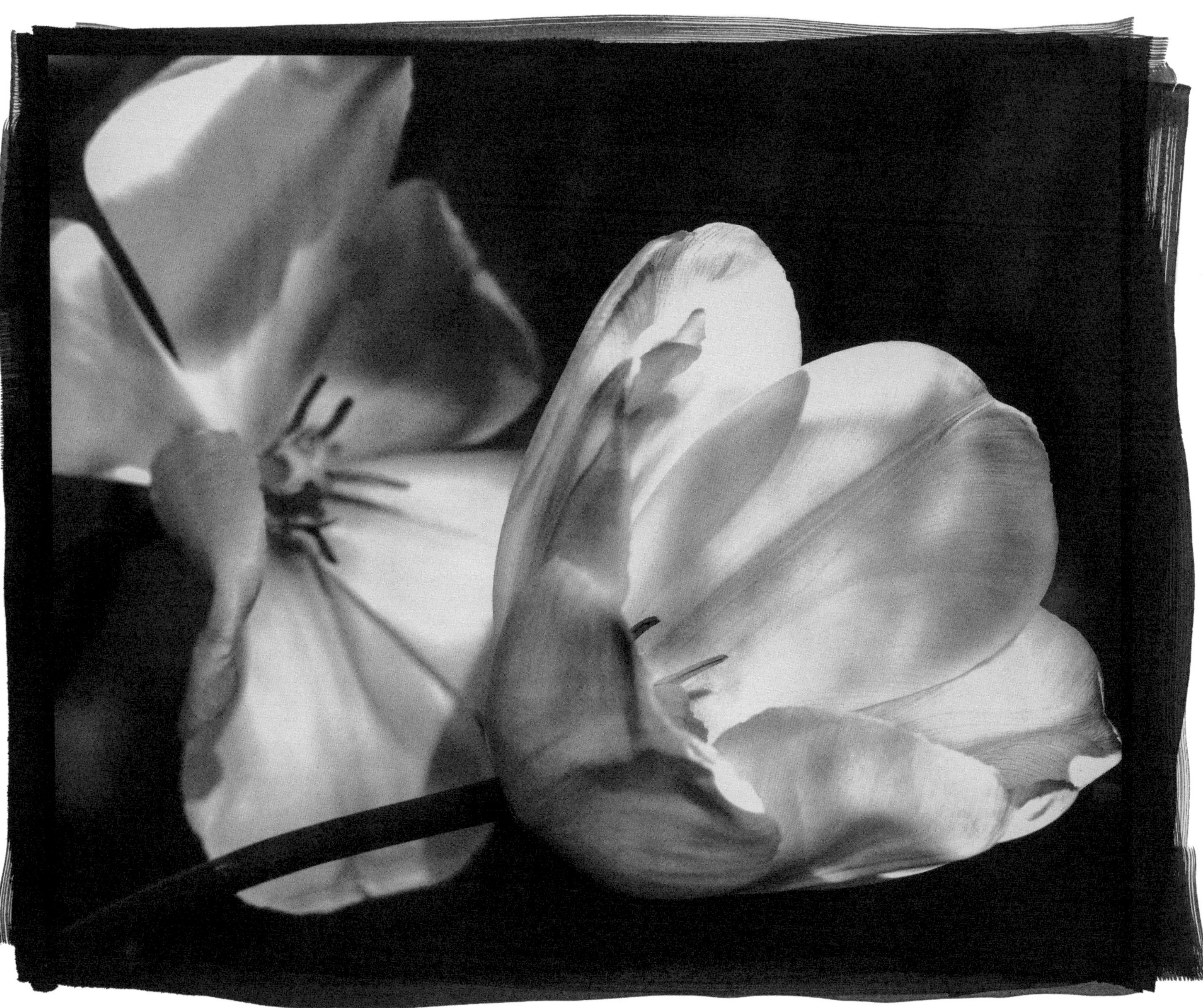

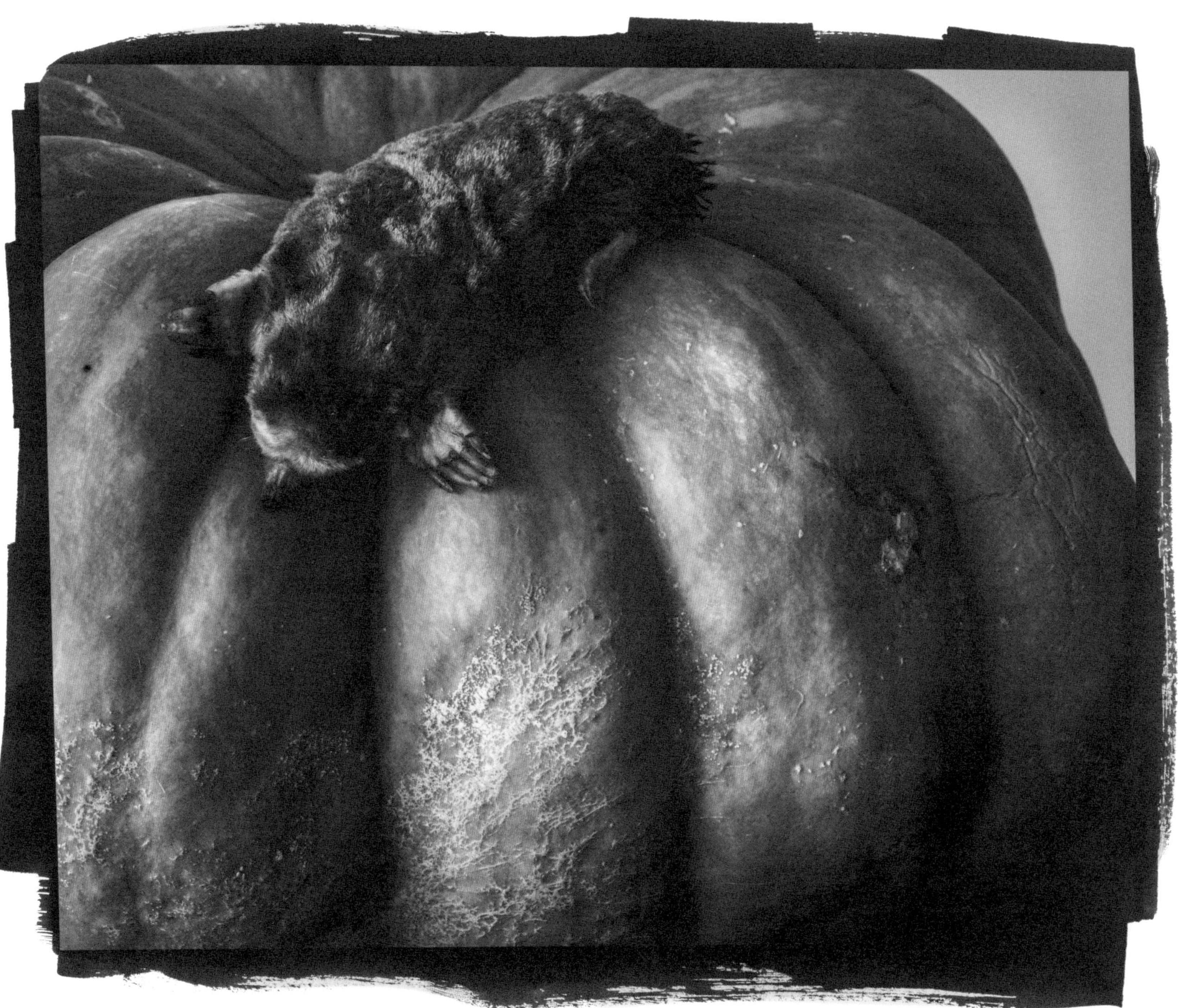

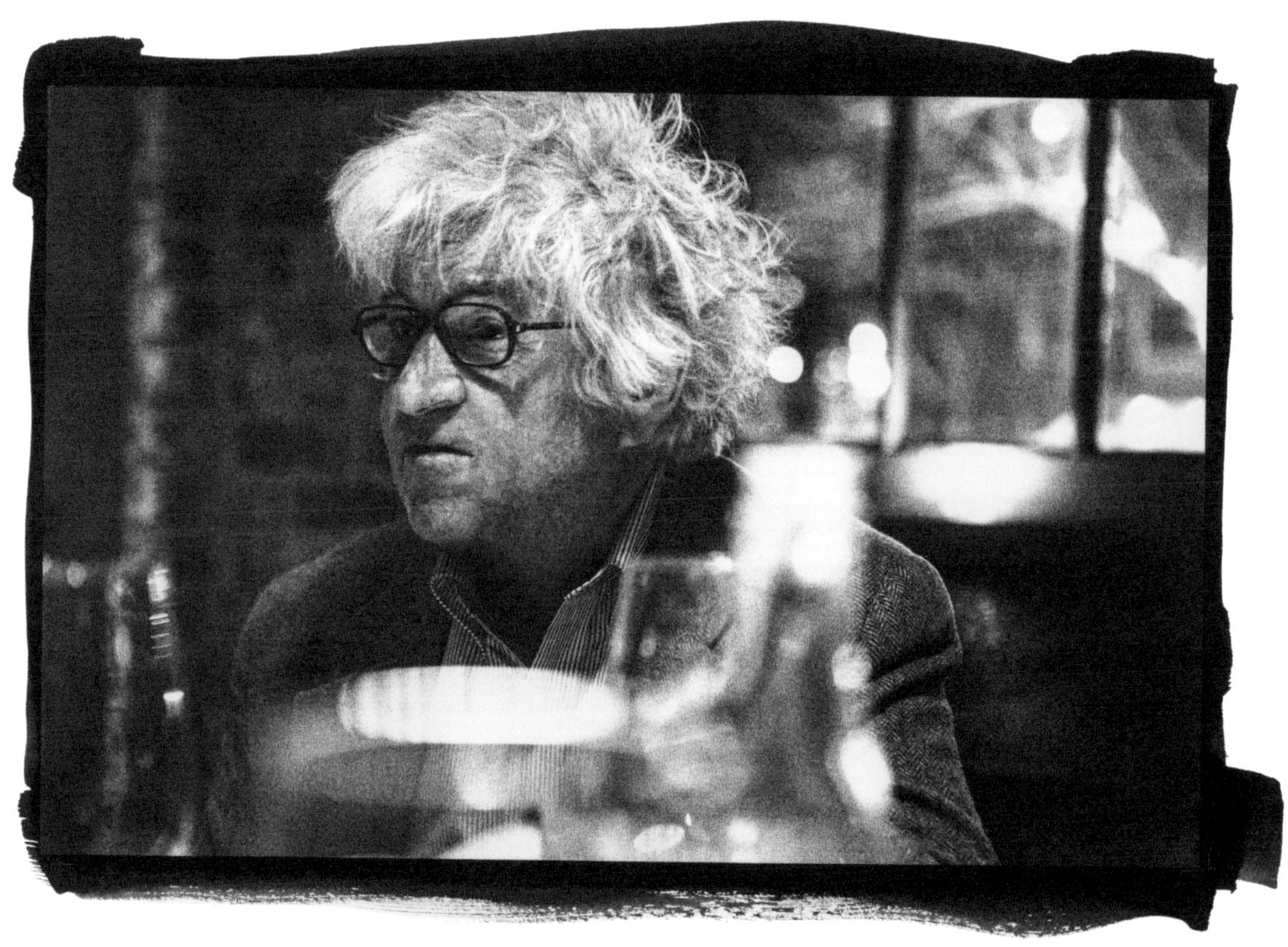

Matthias Harder

VON EINER BÜHNE ZUR ANDEREN. EIN LEBEN FÜR DIE KUNST

Vera Mercer bezeichnete einmal ihren Vater Franz Mertz, einen bedeutenden Bühnenbildner, als ihren wohl wichtigsten künstlerischen Einfluss. 1936 in Berlin geboren, ließ sie sich nach der Schulzeit im modernen Tanz von einem Mary-Wigman-Schüler ausbilden. Über die enge Verbindung zum Theater lernte sie Daniel Spoerri kennen, der damals ebenfalls Tänzer und Regieassistent war; sie begegneten einander in Darmstadt am Landestheater, wo Veras Vater als Bühnenbildner engagiert war. Nach ihrer Hochzeit zogen sie 1958 nach Paris, wo sie in der Künstlergruppe um die „Nouveaux Réalistes" zahlreiche Freunde fanden. Diese benötigten eine fotografische Dokumentation ihrer Werke und Aktionen, und Vera Mertz-Spoerri, wie sie damals hieß, begann eine umfangreiche Aufnahmereihe der künstlerischen Avantgarde in Paris, die dann jahrzehntelang im Archiv schlummerte und erst 2014 in der Publikation „Particular Portraits" mündete. Nach der Trennung von Spoerri fotografierte sie für das Magazin „Theater heute" und kooperierte zudem mit dem dänischen Journalisten und späteren Filmemacher Claus Weeke für skandinavische Zeitschriften, die ihre Porträts von Samuel Beckett, Eugène Ionesco, Norman Mailer, Andy Warhol oder Marcel Duchamp veröffentlichten. Später assistierte sie dem Schweizer Modefotografen Peter Knapp, einem Freund von Spoerri.

Anfang der 1960er-Jahre begann Vera Mercer systematisch die Gemälde und Skulpturen der Basler Künstlerin Eva Aeppli zu dokumentieren, 1984 fanden die Aufnahmen Eingang in eine große Aeppli-Monografie. Über ihre Freundschaft mit der Künstlerin, der früheren Partnerin von Jean Tinguely und späteren

FROM ONE STAGE TO ANOTHER. A LIFE OF ART

Vera Mercer once described her father Franz Mertz, an esteemed stage designer, as her most important artistic influence. Born in Berlin in 1936, after secondary school she trained in modern dance under a student of Mary Wigman. Through her close ties to the world of theater she met Daniel Spoerri, also a dancer as well as an assistant director; they met in Darmstadt at the Landestheater, where Vera's father was engaged as a stage designer. After their marriage they relocated to Paris in 1958, where many of their friends were proponents of the Nouveaux Réalisme art movement. Requiring photographic documentation of their works and happenings, Vera Mertz-Spoerri, as she was known at the time, produced an extensive series of photographs of the artistic avant-garde in Paris. These lay untouched in her archives for decades, until their publication under the title *Particular Portraits* in 2014. After her separation from Spoerri, Vera Mercer worked as a photographer for the magazine *Theater heute* and collaborated with the Danish journalist and later filmmaker, Claus Weeke, for various Scandinavian magazines, which published her portraits of Samuel Beckett, Eugène Ionesco, Norman Mailer, Andy Warhol, and Marcel Duchamp. Later she assisted the Swiss fashion photographer Peter Knapp, a friend of Spoerri.

In the early 1960s, Mercer began documenting the paintings and sculptures of the Swiss artist Eva Aeppli; in 1984 these photographs were included in a major monograph of Aeppli's work. Through her friendship with Aeppli, who was Jean Tinguely's former partner and later Samuel Mercer's wife, Vera met Mercer's son, Mark Mercer. The two traveled by bus and

Frau von Samuel Mercer, lernte Vera dessen Sohn Mark Mercer kennen. Die beiden reisten 1970 für einige Monate von Paris per Bus und Zug nach Indien und anschließend nach Omaha, Nebraska, wo sie sich seitdem des Old Markets, eines Ensembles aus alten Lagerhäusern, annahmen – und dort heirateten. Als Projektentwickler des Old Markets fungierten Samuel und Mark Mercer sowie Nicholas Bonham-Carter; Vera sorgte unter anderem für die Ausstattung. Eine große Fotowand mit Vera Mercers Motiven aus „Les Halles", ihrer Dokumentation der alten Pariser Markthallen, wurde beispielsweise im Restaurant „French Café" in Omaha installiert und später durch Motive aus französischen Cafés ersetzt. Diese Idee einer innenarchitektonischen Raumgestaltung mit großen Fotowänden konnte sie – vermittelt durch John Morford, dem Innenausstatter verschiedener Hyatt-Hotels – auch in Hongkong, Seoul und Tokio realisieren. Die Mercers gründeten zudem zahlreiche andere Restaurants in Omaha, deren Geschicke Vera bis heute lenkt, auch nach dem Tod ihres Ehemanns Mark im Jahr 2019.
Seit 2004 arbeitet Vera Mercer an ihren großformatigen Stillleben, abwechselnd in Omaha und Paris. Diese wurden seitdem immer wieder in unterschiedlichsten Kontexten international ausgestellt und über ihre Galerien in bedeutende Sammlungen vermittelt. Begleitend entstanden drei monografische Publikationen, die im Kehrer- bzw. im Distanz-Verlag erschienen. Die vorliegende neueste Monografie veröffentlicht erstmals Reproduktionen ihrer jüngsten fototechnischen Volte, den Platinum-Prints, denen sie sich seit einigen Jahren intensiv widmet. Zu diesem Zweck hat sich Vera Mercer erneut eine analoge Dunkelkammer eingerichtet, wie vor 60 Jahren in Paris, als sie in erster Linie andere Künstler und deren Werke fotografierte und diese Aufnahmen meist nachts in ihrer Wohnung an der Rue Mouffetard entwickelte. So kehrt Vera Mercer fototechnisch zu ihren Wurzeln zurück. Da aber ihre Kreativität schier unerschöpflich erscheint, können wir gespannt sein, was als nächstes kommt.

train from Paris to India for a few months in 1970 and ultimately ended up in Omaha, Nebraska, where they settled at the Old Market, an ensemble of old warehouses. Samuel and Mark Mercer and Nicholas Bonham-Carter were the project developers for the Old Market; Vera was responsible for the interior, among other things. For example, a large photo wall with Vera Mercer's motifs from her series *Les Halles,* a documentation of the old Parisian market halls, was installed at the French Café restaurant in Omaha. Later, these were replaced by her images of cafés she photographed around France. With the support of John Morford, the interior designer for a number of Hyatt hotels, Mercer was able to take her interior design concept featuring large photo walls to Hong Kong, Seoul, and Tokyo. The Mercers also founded several other restaurants in Omaha, which Vera continues to oversee, even following the death of her husband Mark in 2019.
Vera Mercer has been working on her large-format still lifes since 2004, dividing her time between Omaha and Paris. Since then, her images have been exhibited internationally in a wide variety of contexts, and have been acquired by significant collections through her galleries. Her work has been documented in three monographic publications, published by Kehrer and Distanz. This latest monograph is the first to include reproductions of her platinum prints, produced using a technical process she has been working with intensively for several years now. To do so, Mercer once again set up an analogue darkroom – as she did 60 years ago in Paris – when her primary motifs were other artists and their works, working mostly at night to develop the photographs in her apartment on Rue Mouffetard. Vera Mercer has thus returned to her roots in terms of photographic technology. With her seemingly endless wellspring of creativity, we can look forward to what will come next.

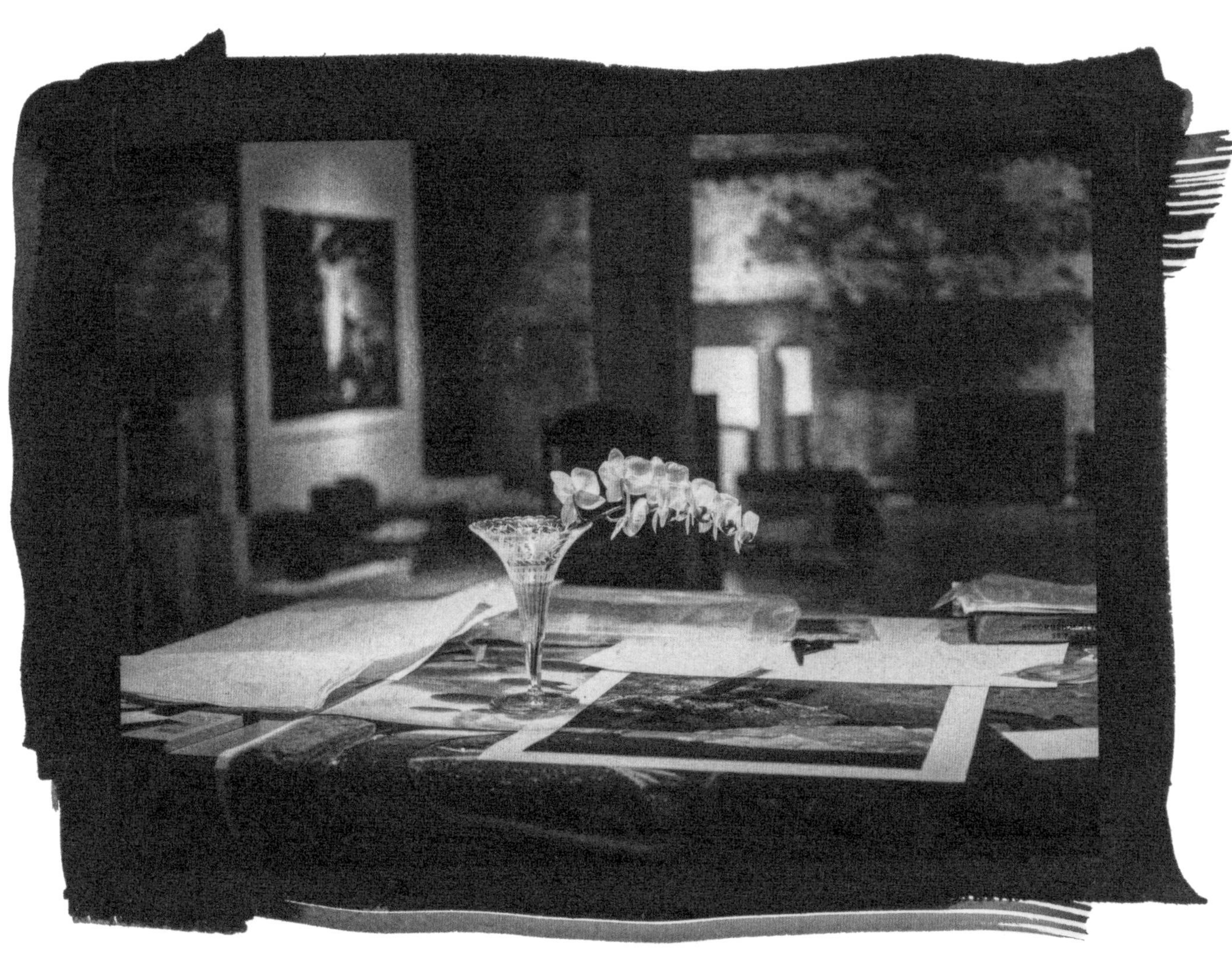

Impressum I Colophon

Herausgeber | Editor
Matthias Harder

Gestaltung | Design
Jonas Kirchner

Texte | Texts
Sergio Fabio Berardini, Matthias Harder

Übersetzung | Translation
Laurence Ferrari/Susanne Hohwieler, Alisa Kotmair

Lektorat | Copy editing
Tanja Vonseelen, Alisa Kotmair

Lithografie | Image editing
DruckConcept, Berlin

Produktion | Production management
DruckConcept, Christiane Rothe, Berlin

Vera Mercer wird vertreten von | is represented by
Galerie Jordanow, Munich
WERKHALLEN Galerie, Kampen/Sylt
Johanna Breede PHOTOKUNST, Berlin
Galerie Schlichtenmaier, Stuttgart
SHERRY LEEDY CONTEMPORARY, Kansas City
CLAIRbyKahn, München, Zürich

Mit besonderen Dank an | Many thanks to
Matthias Harder, Sergio Fabrio Berardini, Uta Grosenick, Elka Jordanow, Christian Rothmann und | and Christiane Rothe

Vertrieb und Marketing I Distribution and marketing
DCV
sales@dcv-books.com

ISBN 978-3-96912-049-1
Printed in Germany

Erschienen bei | Published by

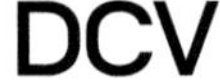

www.dcv-books.com